IFRSs – A Visual Approach

IFRSs – A Visual Approach

Edited by

KPMG Deutsche Treuhand-Gesellschaft
Aktiengesellschaft Wirtschaftsprüfungsgesellschaft

Third Edition

palgrave
macmillan

English Language Translation © Palgrave Macmillan 2008

Originally published as KPMG Deutsche Treuhand-Gesellschaft
Aktiengesellschaft Wirtschaftsprüfungsgesellschaft (Hrsg.)
IFRS Visuell
Die IFRS in strukturierten Übersichten
3., aktualisierte und überarbeitete Auflage
(IFRS as at 10 January 2008)
Copyright © 2008 Schäffer-Poeschel Verlag für Wirtschaft Steuern Recht GmbH
Published by arrangement with Schäffer-Poeschel Verlag GmbH

English translation by Robin Bonthrone (Fry & Bonthrone Partnerschaft, Mainz-Kastel,
Germany)

First published in English 2008 by
PALGRAVE MACMILLAN
Houndmills, Basingstoke, Hampshire RG21 6XS and
175 Fifth Avenue, New York, N.Y. 10010
Companies and representatives throughout the world

PALGRAVE MACMILLAN is the global academic imprint of the Palgrave
Macmillan division of St. Martin's Press, LLC and of Palgrave Macmillan Ltd.
Macmillan® is a registered trademark in the United States, United Kingdom
and other countries. Palgrave is a registered trademark in the European
Union and other countries.

ISBN-13: 978-0-230-57466-3   hardback
ISBN-10: 0-230-57466-1   hardback

This book is printed on paper suitable for recycling and made from fully
managed and sustained forest sources. Logging, pulping and manufacturing
processes are expected to conform to the environmental regulations of the
country of origin.

A catalogue record for this book is available from the British Library.

A catalog record for this book is available from the Library of Congress.

10   9   8   7   6   5   4   3   2   1
17 16 15 14 13 12 11 10 09 08

Printed and bound in Great Britain by
Cromwell Press Ltd, Trowbridge, Wiltshire

Preface

Since 2005, *International Financial Reporting Standards* (IFRSs) have become widely adopted around the world and are now required or permitted to be used in more than 100 countries globally.

More countries adopt IFRSs every year, including Brazil, Canada, Japan and India, which have all announced that they will either converge with or transition to IFRSs over the coming years. In the United States of America, the Securities and Exchange Commission (SEC) has dropped the requirement for foreign entities applying IFRSs to reconcile their financial statements to US GAAP with effect from 15 November 2007. Following consultations in 2007, the SEC is contemplating whether US domestic filers should also be permitted or required to apply IFRSs in place of US GAAP.

The SEC's acknowledgement that IFRSs may be used in place of US GAAP by foreign filers was preceded by efforts by the IASB and its US equivalent, the FASB, to converge US GAAP and IFRSs and remove some of the more significant differences between them. As a result of this convergence agenda, a number of new or amended standards have been issued by the IASB. In addition, the interpretive body of the IASB, the International Financial Reporting Interpretations Committee (IFRIC) has issued new Interpretations with the objective of improving the consistency of the application of IFRSs.

As IFRSs have evolved, both the standards and their application have become increasingly complicated.

This publication provides a simplified summary of the main elements of IFRSs. In part I, simple diagrams based on the layout of financial statements show which of the chronologically numbered standards (IAS 1 to 41 and IFRS 1 to 8) affects each line in the financial statements. Part II summarises each of those standards in a diagram, helping the reader to visualise the key decisions and choices that their application requires. References to relevant paragraphs in the standards are included to allow readers to easily locate further detail and guidance.

The diagrams do not cover every condition, exception or exemption and reference to the standards themselves will always be necessary. However, its simplified structure makes this publication an excellent introduction to IFRSs for those seeking a high level overview and a readily accessible guide to the standards for those wanting to enhance their understanding. By incorporating references to the standards, it provides a quick tool to allow more experienced users to quickly identify relevant guidance.

Students, those involved in the preparation of financial statements, CFOs, non-executive directors, business journalists, management consultants and many others may find this publication of use. Even advanced users wishing to keep abreast of the most recent developments will find that the guide allows them to quickly focus their further research.

IFRSs – A Visual Approach is based on those IFRSs issued by the IASB at 10 January 2008. A number of the more recent developments are not yet currently effective and the text highlights when they are required to be applied for the first time. These effective dates do not address endorsement processes or convergence processes in particular jurisdictions (such as that used in the European Union). As always, care is needed to identify the particular standards and interpretations that are required in your particular jurisdiction.

This publication is the first English translation of a German-language publication prepared by KPMG in Germany that is now in its third edition.

Special thanks go to WP StB Ingo Rahe, who played the lead role in compiling this edition. In addition to the contributors to the previous German editions, we would like to thank Dr Nadine Antonakopoulos, WP StB Jörg Fuhrländer, WP StB Wolfgang Laubauch, WP Carsten Nölgen CPA, WP StB Timo Pütz, WP Charlotte Salzmann CPA, WP StB Jürgen Schneider, Heiko Spang, WP StB Wolfgang Wendholt and WP StB Jörg Wiegand for their valuable contributions to the third German edition on which this English version is based. We would also like to thank Colin Edwards ACA, David Littleford FCA and Anita Romann for their contributions to the English translation.

KPMG also has a wide range of publications that can assist you further with the application of IFRSs, including *Insights into IFRS: KPMG's Practical Guide to International Financial Reporting Standards*, illustrative financial statements and disclosure checklists. Technical information and a briefing on KPMG's IFRS conversion support are available at www.kpmgifrg.com.

For access to an extensive range of accounting, auditing and financial reporting guidance and literature, visit KPMG's Accounting Research Online. This Web-based subscription service can be a valuable tool for anyone who wants to stay informed in today's dynamic environment. For a free 15-day trial, go to www.aro.kpmg.com and register today.

Berlin, May 2008

Contents

List of abbreviations

App.   Appendix

CFO   Chief Financial Officer
CGU   Cash-generating unit

DBO   Defined benefit obligation

EPIS   Earnings per incremental share
EU   European Union

F   Framework
FIFO   First-in, first-out

GAAP   Generally accepted accounting principles

IAS(s)   International Accounting Standard(s)
IASB   International Accounting Standards Board
IFRIC   International Financial Reporting Interpretations Committee
IFRS(s)   International Financial Reporting Standard(s)

POS   Potential ordinary shares

SIC   Standing Interpretations Committee
SPE   Special purpose entity

Disclaimer/clarification

This publication includes a summary of the key requirements of IFRSs. Because it is summarised, it does not include all of the detailed guidance, conditions, or requirements of the Standards. In many instances, further interpretation will be needed in order for an entity to apply IFRSs to its own facts, circumstances and individual transactions. Users are cautioned to read this publication in conjunction with the actual text of the Standards and implementation guidance issued and to consult their professional advisers before concluding on accounting treatments for their own transactions.

I. Introduction

This introduction provides a brief overview of how the pronouncements included within this publication are presented.

The publication covers all of the International Accounting Standards (IASs) and International Financial Reporting Standards (IFRSs) issued by the IASB as at 10 January 2008 as well as the Interpretations issued by the IFRIC at that date.

The numbering of the pronouncements has developed over time and does not relate to their content. The first part of this guide presents a simplified overview of how the Standards relate to the individual line items in the financial statements.

The second part of the guide sets out a summary of each of the Standards and Interpretations. Each pronouncement is introduced by a short narrative description which includes a summary of its core principles, its scope (including any scope exclusions) and its effective date. For each Interpretation, a summary of the Standards to which it relates is also included. In principle, all Standards and Interpretations must be applied by all entities. Exceptions to this rule relate to IAS 14/IFRS 8 and IAS 33, which need only be applied by publicly traded entities.

Each introduction is followed by diagrams that provide focussed summaries of the interrelationships between the core content of the Standards. As far as possible, these illustrations distinguish between the core principles and exceptions. Options and alternative accounting treatments explicitly permitted by the standards are highlighted[1]. To ensure that the publication focuses on the core elements of the Standards, we have made a conscious decision not to highlight all aspects of every principle or exception. Readers wanting a more detailed insight as well as a rationale for the decisions made by the IASB on how to account for specific matters should consult the original Standards and Interpretations and, if necessary, a relevant commentary on IFRSs.

The diagrammatic illustrations are generally based on the structure of the Standard or Interpretation concerned. Topics that are explained in greater detail on following pages are identified by a symbol linking to the corresponding page.

References to the Standards and Interpretations have been included in the illustrations to allow more detailed research. For example, the first illustration of IAS 2 contains a box labelled 'Costs of purchase (11)'. This means that the requirements governing the purchase costs of inventories are contained in paragraph 11 of IAS 2.

---

1 Note: Many of the options and exceptions included within the Standards may only be used in specific or limited circumstances. Readers should consult the actual text of the Standards to determine whether a specific option or exception may be applied in any given situation.

As a rule, we have not described the disclosures required in the notes unless the standard in question only addresses disclosure.

Readers are reminded that the terminology used in this publication relates to the Standards and Interpretations in issue as at 10 January 2008. Certain accounting terms that were commonly used in previous versions of IFRSs have been superseded in the course of the IASB/FASB convergence process. Examples of such terms include 'statement of financial position' (formerly 'balance sheet'), 'statement of comprehensive income' (formerly 'income statement'), 'statement of cash flows' (formerly 'cash flow statement'), 'non-controlling interests' (formerly 'minority interests') and 'end of (the) reporting period' (formerly 'balance sheet date' or 'reporting date').

Allocation of Standards to Financial Statement Line Items (1/5): Statement of Financial Position

Primary standards:

IAS 1 · IAS 8 · IAS 10 · IAS 17 · IAS 20 · IAS 21 · IAS 23 · IAS 27 · IAS 31
IFRS 1 · IFRS 2 · IFRS 3 · IFRS 4 · IFRS 6

ASSETS

IAS 16+36	Property, plant and equipment
IAS 40	Investment property
IAS 38+36	Intangible assets
IAS 39	Financial assets
IAS 28	Equity-accounted investments
IAS 41	Biological assets
IAS 2+11	Inventories
IAS 39	Trade and other receivables
IAS 39	Cash and cash equivalents
IAS 12	Current tax assets
IAS 12	Deferred tax assets
IFRS 5	Non-current assets and disposal groups held for sale

EQUITY AND LIABILITIES

Standard	Line item
IAS 1+27+32	Equity attributable to equity holders of the parent
IAS 27	Non-controlling interests (presented within equity)
IAS 19+37	Provisions
IAS 39	Financial liabilities
IAS 39	Other liabilities
IAS 12	Current tax liabilities
IAS 12	Deferred tax liabilities
IFRS 5	Liabilities directly associated with non-current assets and disposal groups held for sale

KPMG

Allocation of Standards to Financial Statement Line Items (2/5): Statement of Comprehensive Income

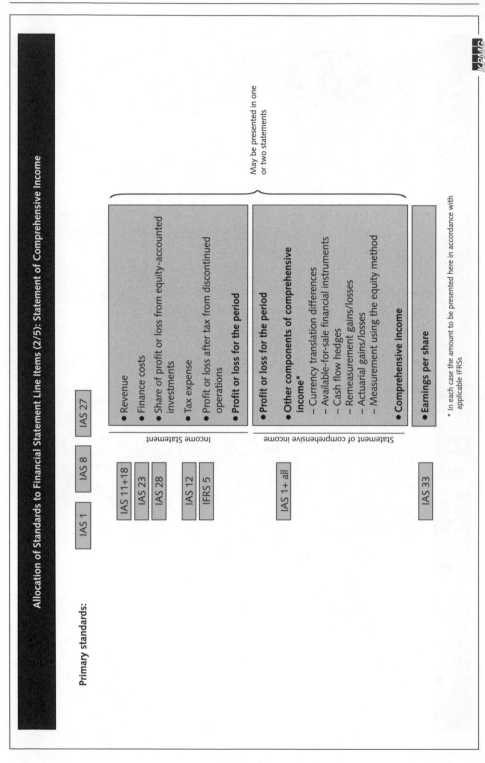

Primary standards:

IAS 1   IAS 8   IAS 27

Income Statement

IAS 11+18
IAS 23
IAS 28

IAS 12
IFRS 5

- Revenue
- Finance costs
- Share of profit or loss from equity-accounted investments
- Tax expense
- Profit or loss after tax from discontinued operations
- **Profit or loss for the period**

Statement of comprehensive income

IAS 1+ all

- **Profit or loss for the period**
- **Other components of comprehensive income***
  - Currency translation differences
  - Available-for-sale financial instruments
  - Cash flow hedges
  - Remeasurement gains/losses
  - Actuarial gains/losses
  - Measurement using the equity method
- **Comprehensive income**

May be presented in one or two statements

IAS 33

- **Earnings per share**

* In each case the amount to be presented here in accordance with applicable IFRSs

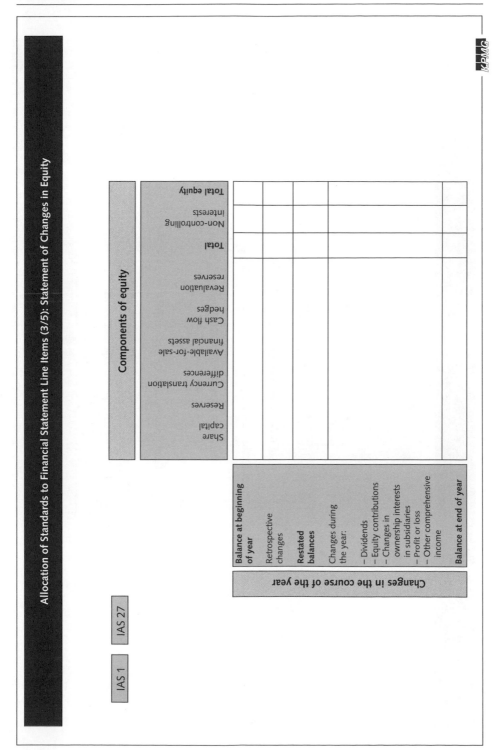

Allocation of Standards to Financial Statement Line Items (3/5): Statement of Changes in Equity

IAS 1 IAS 27

Components of equity

	Share capital	Reserves	Currency translation differences	Available-for-sale financial assets	Cash flow hedges	Revaluation reserves	Total	Non-controlling interests	Total equity

Changes in the course of the year

- Balance at beginning of year
- Retrospective changes
- **Restated balances**
- Changes during the year:
  - Dividends
  - Equity contributions
  - Changes in ownership interests in subsidiaries
  - Profit or loss
  - Other comprehensive income
- Balance at end of year

Allocation of Standards to Financial Statement Line Items (4/5): Statement of Cash Flows

IAS 7

Statement of cash flows

Sources and application of funds

Cash flows from operating activities

Cash flows from investing activities

Cash flows from financing activities

Effect of exchange rate changes on cash and cash equivalents

Net change in cash and cash equivalents

KPMG

Allocation of Standards to Financial Statement Line Items (5/5): Notes

Primary standards:

IAS 1

- Basis of preparation and accounting policies applied
- Supplementary information on financial statement items required by other Standards
- Additional information required by other Standards
- Disclosures on statement of cash flows
- Segment reporting

All

All

IAS 37 + IFRS 7

IAS 7

IFRS 8

Segment reporting

Segment
I II III IV Group

A
B
C
D

IAS 1

Additional disclosures:
- on capital
- on dividends declared or proposed after the reporting date
- on sources of estimation uncertainty
- on the entity

Typical Structure of a Standard

Typical structure of a standard

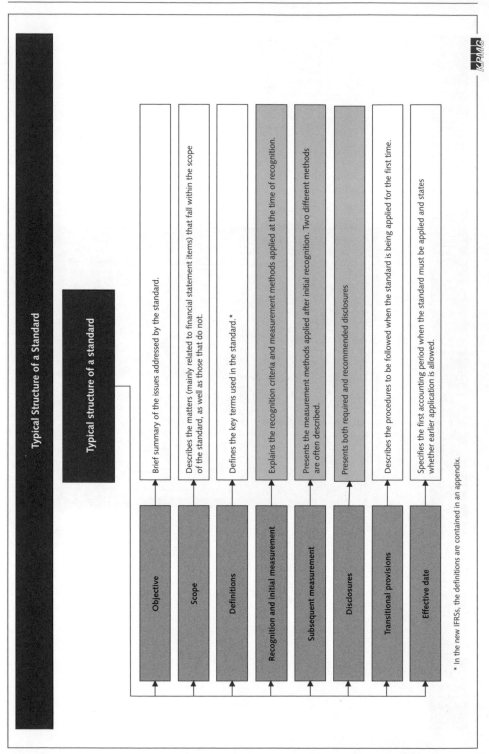

Objective	Brief summary of the issues addressed by the standard.
Scope	Describes the matters (mainly related to financial statement items) that fall within the scope of the standard, as well as those that do not.
Definitions	Defines the key terms used in the standard.*
Recognition and initial measurement	Explains the recognition criteria and measurement methods applied at the time of recognition.
Subsequent measurement	Presents the measurement methods applied after initial recognition. Two different methods are often described.
Disclosures	Presents both required and recommended disclosures
Transitional provisions	Describes the procedures to be followed when the standard is being applied for the first time.
Effective date	Specifies the first accounting period when the standard must be applied and states whether earlier application is allowed.

* In the new IFRSs, the definitions are contained in an appendix.

II. The International Financial Reporting Standards

IAS 1 Presentation of Financial Statements
(amended 2008)

Scope:	Overall requirements for the preparation and presentation of financial statements
Scope exclusions:	–
Core principles:	A set of financial statements comprises a statement of financial position, a statement of comprehensive income, a statement of changes in equity, a statement of cash flows and notes.
	An entity may optionally present the statement of comprehensive income in one statement or two statements.
	Financial statements must reflect the following overall considerations. They must present fairly the financial position, financial performance and cash flows of the entity. Management must assess the entity's ability to continue as a going concern. Except for the statement of cash flows, the entity must prepare its financial statements using the accrual basis of accounting. The presentation and classification of items in the financial statements must be consistent from one period to the next. Each material item must be presented separately in the financial statements. Assets and liabilities may only be offset if explicitly required or permitted by another standard. As a rule, comparative information must be disclosed in respect of the previous period(s) presented for all amounts reported in the financial statements. In special cases (a retrospective change due to a new or amended accounting policy, error correction, or reclassification), an additional statement of financial position must be prepared for the beginning of the first previous period presented.
Effective date:	Annual periods beginning on or after 1 January 2009. Earlier application is permitted. Amendments resulting from IAS 27 (amended 2008) must be applied at the same time as the amended IAS 27.
Applies to:	All entities

IAS 1 Presentation of Financial Statements (1/7)

Components of financial statements

The titles of the components may differ from those used in IAS 1 (10)

1. Statement of financial position (10 (a))
2. Statement of comprehensive income (10 (b))
3. Statement of changes in equity (10 (c))
4. Statement of cash flows (10 (d))
5. Notes (10 (e))

Required components of financial statements

6. Statement of financial position as at the beginning of the earliest comparative period (10 (f))

Additional component required if items are reclassified or restated retrospectively, or if there is a retrospective change in accounting policy

Management report on the position of the entity (13)

Environmental report (14)

Value added statement (14)

Possible components; presented outside the financial statements

KPMG

IAS 1 Presentation of Financial Statements (2/7)

Overall considerations

Compliance with all standards

If all standards are applied, the financial position, financial performance and cash flows of an entity are presumed to be presented fairly. In extremely rare circumstances in which departure from the requirements of a standard is necessary to achieve fair presentation, the question of whether the entity may depart from the requirements of the standard or whether merely a disclosure in the notes is required depends on the applicable regulatory framework. (15–24)

Going concern

Financial statements are prepared on a going concern basis. If the entity will not be continued as a going concern, or if management has no realistic alternative, the financial statements must be prepared on an appropriate basis and this fact must be disclosed. (25–26)

Accrual basis of accounting

Except for the statement of cash flows, the accrual basis of accounting is applied to the assets, liabilities, equity, income and expenses in the financial statements. (27–28)

Materiality and aggregation

Items may be aggregated, provided that material and dissimilar items are presented separately. No disclosures are required in the notes if the information is not material. (29–31)

Offsetting

Offsetting is prohibited unless required or permitted by a standard. (32–35)

Frequency of reporting

An entity must present a complete set of financial statements at least annually. If an entity changes to year end and presents financial statements for a period longer or shorter than one year, it must make additional disclosures. (36–37)

Comparative information

Comparative information is generally required for all amounts reported in the financial statements. Comparative narrative and descriptive information is included if it is relevant to an understanding of the current period. Comparative information must be reclassified if there is a change in presentation in the current period. In special cases (a retrospective change due to a new or amended accounting policy, error correction, or reclassification), an additional statement of financial position must be prepared for the beginning of the first previous period presented. (38–44)

Consistency of presentation

The presentation and classification of items in the financial statements should be consistent from one period to the next unless a different presentation would enhance the quality of information due to a change in the entity's business operations, or a change is required by a standard. (45–46)

KPMG

IAS 1 Presentation of Financial Statements (3/7)

Structure and content

Statement of financial position

- Generally classified by maturity ('current/non-current distinction') unless a liquidity-based classification would provide more relevant information. (60)
- Detailed requirements on classification of assets or liabilities as current or non-current (66–76)
- Minimum content of the statement of financial position (54)
- Disclosures about equity (may be given in the notes) (79–80)

(4/7)

Statement of comprehensive income

- Presented either in one or two statements (81)
- Minimum content of the statement of comprehensive income. Extraordinary items. (82, 83, 87)
- Classified using either the nature or function of expenses. (99)
- Material items are disclosed and described separately. (97)
- Disclosure of certain items that may optionally be presented in the notes. (90, 97, 99)

(5/7)

Statement of changes in equity

- Required columns and lines to be presented (106)
- Separate presentation of total amounts attributable to owners of the parent and to non-controlling interests (106 (a))
- Information on dividends, including dividends per share (may be given optionally in the notes) (107)

(7/7)

Statement of cash flows

- Refer to IAS 7 (111)

Notes

- Statement of compliance with IFRSs (114 (a), 16)
- Significant accounting policies (114 (b), 117)
- Additional disclosures on financial statement line items required by other standards (114 (c))
- Other information required by other standards (114 (d))
- Disclosures on estimation uncertainty, capital, dividends proposed or resolved that are not yet recognised in the financial statements, and the entity. (125, 134, 137, 138)

KPMG

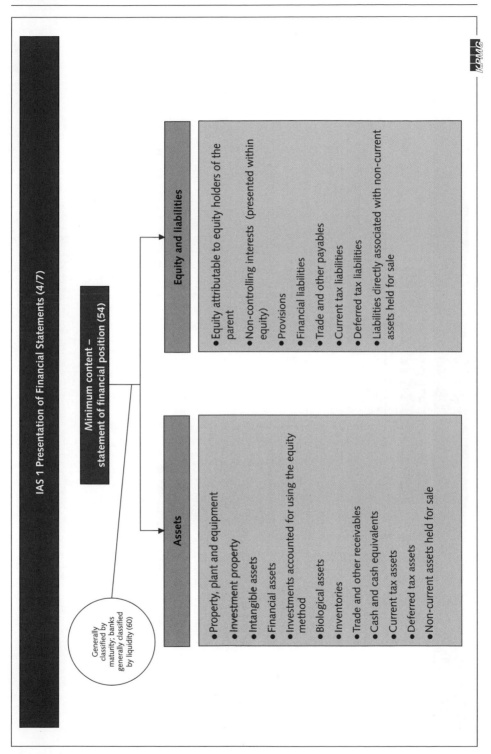

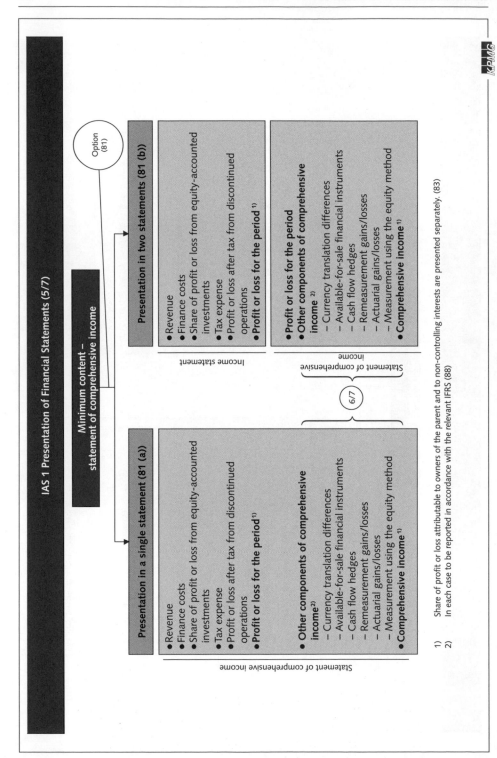

IAS 1 Presentation of Financial Statements (5/7)

**Minimum content –
statement of comprehensive income**

Option
(81)

Presentation in a single statement (81 (a))

- Revenue
- Finance costs
- Share of profit or loss from equity-accounted investments
- Tax expense
- Profit or loss after tax from discontinued operations
- **Profit or loss for the period** [1]

- **Other components of comprehensive income** [2]
  - Currency translation differences
  - Available-for-sale financial instruments
  - Cash flow hedges
  - Remeasurement gains/losses
  - Actuarial gains/losses
  - Measurement using the equity method
- **Comprehensive income** [1]

Statement of comprehensive income

Presentation in two statements (81 (b))

- Revenue
- Finance costs
- Share of profit or loss from equity-accounted investments
- Tax expense
- Profit or loss after tax from discontinued operations
- **Profit or loss for the period** [1]

Income statement

- **Profit or loss for the period**
- **Other components of comprehensive income** [2]
  - Currency translation differences
  - Available-for-sale financial instruments
  - Cash flow hedges
  - Remeasurement gains/losses
  - Actuarial gains/losses
  - Measurement using the equity method
- **Comprehensive income** [1]

Statement of comprehensive income

6/7

1)　Share of profit or loss attributable to owners of the parent and to non-controlling interests are presented separately. (83)
2)　In each case to be reported in accordance with the relevant IFRS (88)

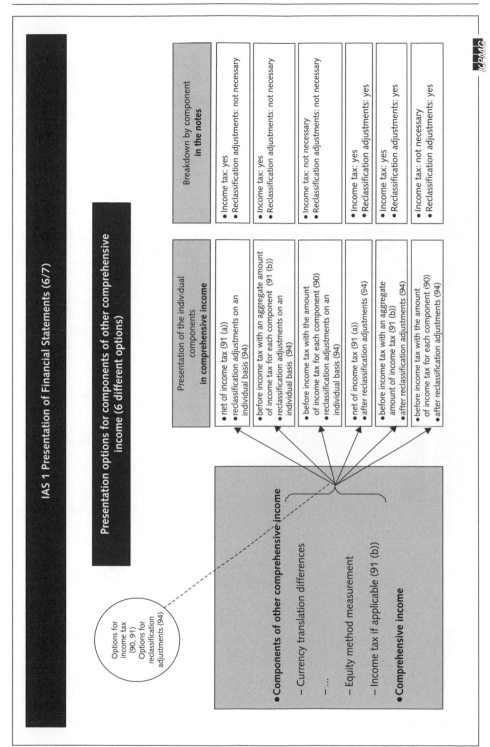

IAS 1 Presentation of Financial Statements (6/7)

Presentation options for components of other comprehensive income (6 different options)

Options for income tax (90, 91)
Options for reclassification adjustments (94)

- **Components of other comprehensive income**
  - Currency translation differences
  - ...
  - Equity method measurement
  - Income tax if applicable (91 (b))
- **Comprehensive income**

Presentation of the individual components **in comprehensive income**

- net of income tax (91 (a))
- reclassification adjustments on an individual basis (94)

- before income tax with an aggregate amount of income tax for each component (91 (b))
- reclassification adjustments on an individual basis (94)

- before income tax with the amount of income tax for each component (90)
- reclassification adjustments on an individual basis (94)

- net of income tax (91 (a))
- after reclassification adjustments (94)

- before income tax with an aggregate amount of income tax (91 (b))
- after reclassification adjustments (94)

- before income tax with the amount of income tax for each component (90)
- after reclassification adjustments (94)

Breakdown by component **in the notes**

- Income tax: yes
- Reclassification adjustments: not necessary

- Income tax: yes
- Reclassification adjustments: not necessary

- Income tax: not necessary
- Reclassification adjustments: not necessary

- Income tax: yes
- Reclassification adjustments: yes

- Income tax: yes
- Reclassification adjustments: yes

- Income tax: not necessary
- Reclassification adjustments: yes

KPMG

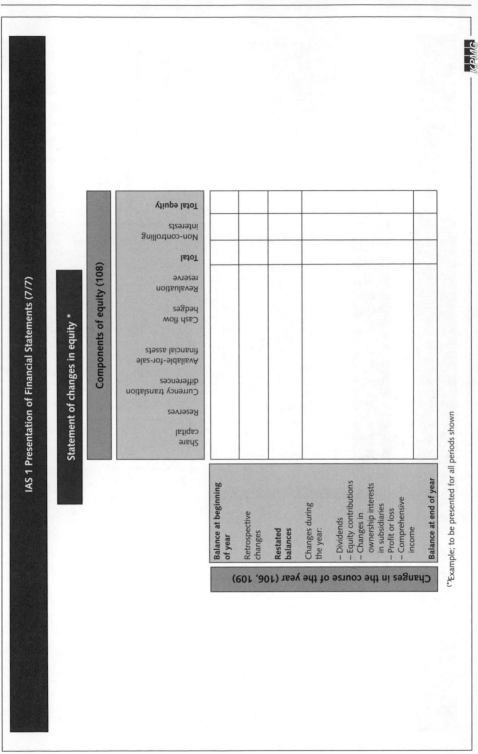

IAS 1 Presentation of Financial Statements (7/7)

Statement of changes in equity *

Components of equity (108)

Changes in the course of the year (106, 109)

	Share capital	Reserves	Currency translation differences	Available-for-sale financial assets	Cash flow hedges	Revaluation reserve	Total	Non-controlling interests	Total equity
Balance at beginning of year									
Retrospective changes									
Restated balances									
Changes during the year:									
– Dividends									
– Equity contributions									
– Changes in ownership interests in subsidiaries									
– Profit or loss									
– Comprehensive income									
Balance at end of year									

*Example; to be presented for all periods shown

IAS 2 Inventories (amended 2006)

Scope:	Inventories
Scope exclusions:	Inventories from construction contracts, financial instruments, certain biological assets and certain agricultural produce.
	Also not applicable to the measurement basis of inventories held by certain producers of agricultural and forest producers, biological assets and certain agricultural produce at the point of harvest or inventories held by commodity broker-traders.
Core principles:	Inventories are measured at the lower of cost and net realisable value. In addition to the purchase price, the cost of purchase includes transaction costs and purchase price reductions. In addition to direct labour, the cost of conversion includes all indirect costs directly related to the units of production. IAS 23 requires borrowing costs to be capitalised. The first-in, first-out (FIFO) or weighted average cost formulas are permitted as simplified measurement techniques. Net realisable value is defined as the estimated selling price less the estimated costs of completion and estimated costs necessary to make the sale. In exceptional cases only, replacement cost can be used as a measure of net realisable value. Net realisable value must be reassessed in each subsequent period. If the reasons for previous write-downs no longer exist, the write-down is reversed so that the new carrying amount is the lower of cost and revised net realisable value.
Effective date:	Annual periods beginning on or after 1 January 2005. Earlier application is encouraged.
Applies to:	All entities

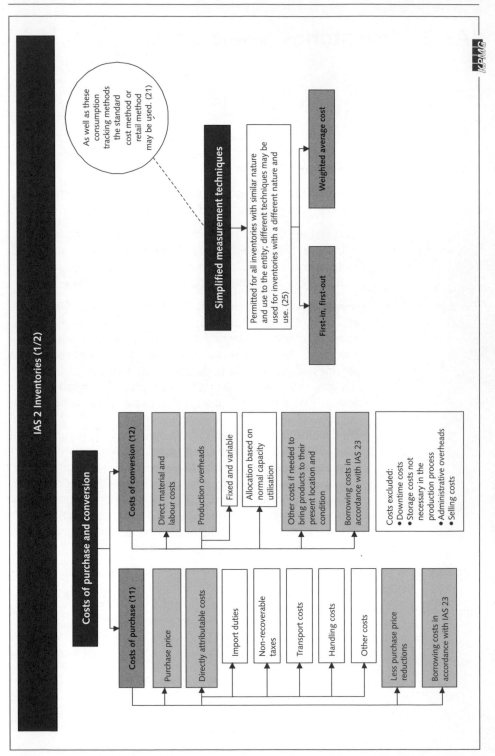

IAS 2 Inventories (1/2)

As well as these consumption tracking methods the standard cost method or retail method may be used. (21)

Simplified measurement techniques

Permitted for all inventories with similar nature and use to the entity; different techniques may be used for inventories with a different nature and use. (25)

Weighted average cost

First-in, first-out

Costs of purchase and conversion

Costs of conversion (12)

Direct material and labour costs

Production overheads

Fixed and variable

Allocation based on normal capacity utilisation

Other costs if needed to bring products to their present location and condition

Borrowing costs in accordance with IAS 23

Costs excluded:
• Downtime costs
• Storage costs not necessary in the production process
• Administrative overheads
• Selling costs

Costs of purchase (11)

Purchase price

Directly attributable costs

Import duties

Non-recoverable taxes

Transport costs

Handling costs

Other costs

Less purchase price reductions

Borrowing costs in accordance with IAS 23

KPMG

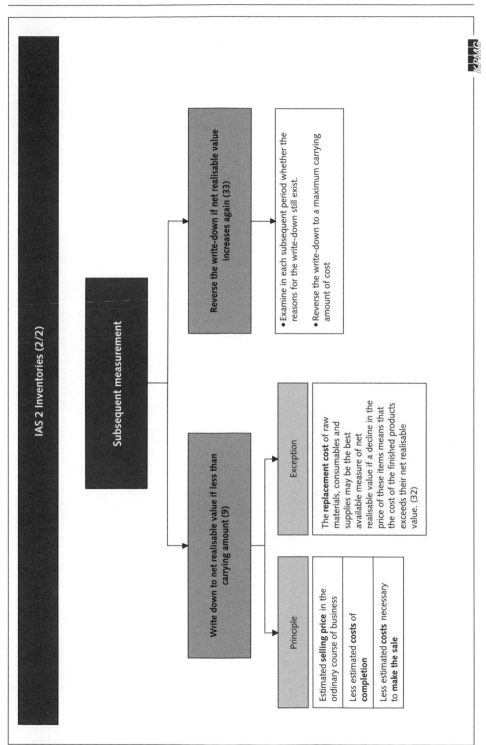

IAS 2 Inventories (2/2)

Subsequent measurement

Write down to net realisable value if less than carrying amount (9)

Principle

Estimated **selling price** in the ordinary course of business

Less estimated **costs of completion**

Less estimated **costs** necessary **to make the sale**

Exception

The **replacement cost** of raw materials, consumables and supplies may be the best available measure of net realisable value if a decline in the price of these items means that the cost of the finished products exceeds their net realisable value. (32)

Reverse the write-down if net realisable value increases again (33)

- Examine in each subsequent period whether the reasons for the write-down still exist.

- Reverse the write-down to a maximum carrying amount of cost

IAS 7 Statement of Cash Flows
(amended 2008)

Scope:	Preparation and presentation of statements of cash flows
Scope exclusions:	–
Core principles:	The statement of cash flows is an integral element of an entity's financial statements. It explains changes in cash and cash equivalents by showing how cash is generated and used.
	In addition to cash (cash on hand and demand deposits), cash and cash equivalents include short-term, highly liquid investments that are readily convertible to cash (cash equivalents). Bank overdrafts that are repayable on demand must be deducted in some cases.
	The statement of cash flows classifies cash flows during the period as arising from operating, investing or financing activities. Cash flows from operating activities can be presented using the direct or the indirect method. Cash flows from interest, dividends and taxes on income may be classified into any one of the three activities, but this classification must then be applied consistently. Unrealised gains/losses arising from changes in exchange rates, the effect on cash and cash equivalents of the acquisition or disposal of subsidiaries and other business units, and non-cash transactions must not be presented as cash flows.
	The effect of unrealised exchange rate gains/losses on cash and cash equivalents is presented separately from the cash flows from operating, investing and financing activities.
	Acquisition/disposals of entities, non-cash transactions and cash and cash equivalents must be explained in the notes to the statement of cash flows.
Effective date:	Annual periods beginning on or after 1 January 1994. Amendments resulting from IAS 27 (amended 2008) must be applied at the same time as the amended IAS 27.
Applies to:	All entities

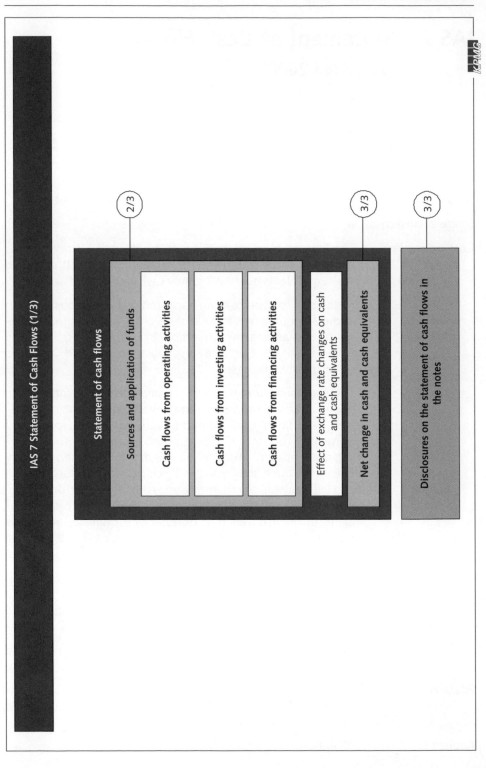

IAS 7 Statement of Cash Flows (1/3)

Statement of cash flows

2/3

Sources and application of funds

Cash flows from operating activities

Cash flows from investing activities

Cash flows from financing activities

Effect of exchange rate changes on cash and cash equivalents

3/3

Net change in cash and cash equivalents

3/3

Disclosures on the statement of cash flows in the notes

KPMG

IAS 7 Statement of Cash Flows (2/3)

Cash flows from operating activities (13–15)

Direct method (19)
- Cash receipts from the sale of goods and the rendering of services
- Cash receipts from royalties, fees, commissions and other revenue
- Cash payments to suppliers
- Cash payments to and on behalf of employees
- Income taxes paid (may optionally be presented in investing activities or financing activities)

Indirect method (20)
- Profit or loss before taxation
- +/– Changes during the period in inventories and operating receivables and payables
- +/– Other non-cash items
- +/– Other items that are assigned to other activities (e.g.: gain or loss on disposal of property, plant and equipment; optional presentation of interest, dividends, taxes on income) (31, 35)

Cash flows from investing activities (16)
- Cash payments to acquire property, plant and equipment, intangibles and other long-term assets
- Cash receipts from sales of property, plant and equipment, intangibles and other long-term assets
- Cash payments to acquire subsidiaries (less cash and cash equivalents acquired)
- Cash receipts from disposals of subsidiaries (less cash and cash equivalents disposed)
- Cash payments for other financial assets
- Cash receipts from other financial assets
- (Optional presentation of interest, dividends and taxes on income) (31, 35)

Cash flows from financing activities (17)
- Cash proceeds from issuing shares or other equity instruments
- Repayments of capital to owners
- Cash proceeds from issuing financial liabilities
- Cash repayments for financial liabilities
- Cash payments to reduce outstanding finance lease liabilities
- Cash flows arising from changes in ownership interests in subsidiaries that do not result in a loss of control (42A)
- (Optional presentation of interest, dividends and taxes on income) (31,35)

Effect of exchange rate changes on cash and cash equivalents (28)
- Unrealised gains/losses arising from changes in exchange rates affecting cash and cash equivalents held.

IAS 7 Statement of Cash Flows (3/3)

Cash and cash equivalents

Cash (6)
- Cash on hand and demand deposits

Cash equivalents (7–9)
- are readily convertible to known amounts of cash
- are only subject to an insignificant risk of change in value; therefore they may only have an original maturity on acquisition of three months or less.
- Bank borrowings are deducted if they are repayable on demand and form an integral part of an entitys cash management (e.g. bank overdrafts)

Disclosures

Acquisitions and disposals of subsidiaries and other business units (40)
- The total purchase or disposal consideration
- The portion of the purchase or disposal consideration discharged by means of cash and cash equivalents
- The amount of cash and cash equivalents in the subsidiary or business unit acquired or disposed of
- The amount of the assets and liabilities other than cash or cash equivalents in the subsidiary or business unit acquired or disposed of, summarised by each major category

Non-cash transactions, e.g.: (43, 44)
- The acquisition of assets either by assuming directly related liabilities or by means of a finance lease
- The acquisition of an entity by means of an equity issue
- The conversion of debt into equity

Cash and cash equivalents (45)
- Components of cash and cash equivalents
- Reconciliation to the statement of financial position
- Restricted cash and cash equivalent balances

KPMG

IAS 8 Accounting Policies, Changes in Accounting Estimates and Errors
(amended 2007)

Scope:	Selection and application of accounting policies; accounting for changes in accounting policies, changes in accounting estimates and corrections of prior-period errors.
Scope exclusions:	–
Core principles:	Accounting policies are applied using the relevant standards and interpretations. If specific guidance is lacking, the requirements and guidance in other standards and interpretations dealing with similar issues, the Framework, or recent pronouncements issued by other standard-setters must be considered. The policies must be applied consistently. Accounting policies may only be changed if the change is required by a standard or interpretation or if it results in reliable and more relevant information being presented.
	Changes in accounting policies and corrections of errors are generally applied retrospectively. This means that the financial statements must be prepared as if the new or correct accounting policy had always been applied. Comparative amounts must be adjusted, but only to the extent that retrospective application is practicable.
	In contrast, changes in accounting estimates are applied prospectively from the date of the change of the estimate to the current and future periods. Prior-period comparative amounts are not adjusted.
Effective date:	Annual periods beginning on or after 1 January 2005. Earlier application is encouraged.
Applies to:	All entities

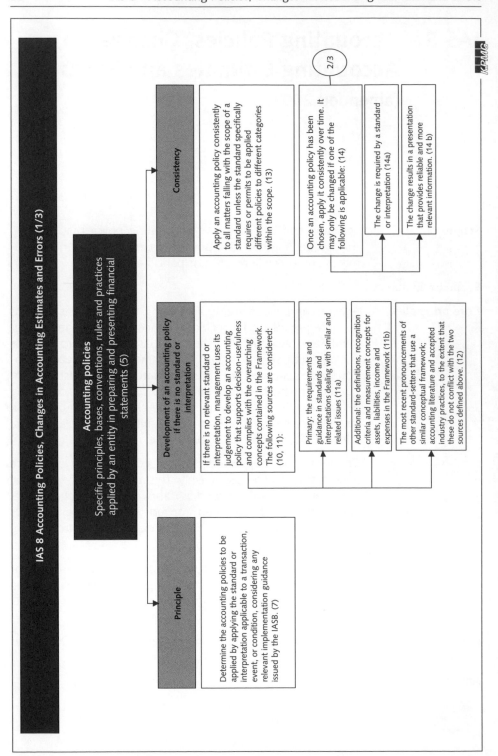

IAS 8 Accounting Policies, Changes in Accounting Estimates and Errors (1/3)

Accounting policies

Specific principles, bases, conventions, rules and practices applied by an entity in preparing and presenting financial statements (5)

Principle

Determine the accounting policies to be applied by applying the standard or interpretation applicable to a transaction, event, or condition, considering any relevant implementation guidance issued by the IASB. (7)

Development of an accounting policy if there is no standard or interpretation

If there is no relevant standard or interpretation, management uses its judgement to develop an accounting policy that supports decision-usefulness and complies with the overarching concepts contained in the Framework. The following sources are considered: (10, 11):

Primary: the requirements and guidance in standards and interpretations dealing with similar and related issues (11a)

Additional: the definitions, recognition criteria and measurement concepts for assets, liabilities, income and expenses in the Framework (11b)

The most recent pronouncements of other standard-setters that use a similar conceptual framework; accounting literature and accepted industry practices, to the extent that these do not conflict with the two sources defined above. (12)

Consistency

Apply an accounting policy consistently to all matters falling with the scope of a standard unless the standard specifically requires or permits to be applied different policies to different categories within the scope. (13)

Once an accounting policy has been chosen, apply it consistently over time. It may only be changed if one of the following is applicable: (14)

The change is required by a standard or interpretation (14a)

The change results in a presentation that provides reliable and more relevant information. (14 b)

2/3

KPMG

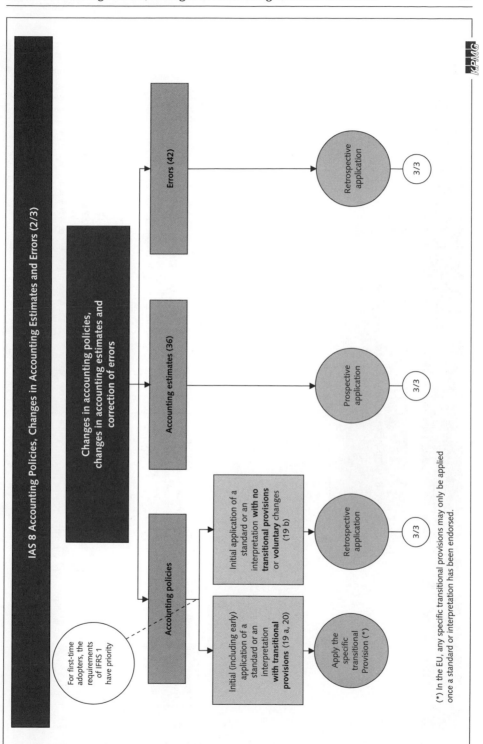

IAS 8 Accounting Policies, Changes in Accounting Estimates and Errors (2/3)

Changes in accounting policies, changes in accounting estimates and correction of errors

For first-time adopters, the requirements of IFRS 1 have priority

Accounting policies

Accounting estimates (36)

Errors (42)

Initial (including early) application of a standard or an interpretation **with transitional provisions** (19 a, 20)

Initial application of a standard or an interpretation **with no transitional provisions** or **voluntary** changes (19 b)

Apply the specific transitional Provision (*)

Retrospective application

3/3

Prospective application

3/3

Retrospective application

3/3

(*) In the EU, any specific transitional provisions may only be applied once a standard or interpretation has been endorsed.

KPMG

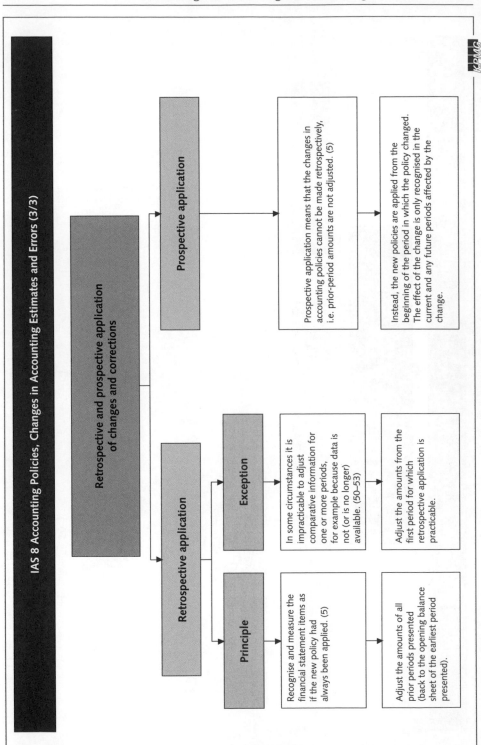

IAS 8 Accounting Policies, Changes in Accounting Estimates and Errors (3/3)

Retrospective and prospective application of changes and corrections

Retrospective application

Principle

Recognise and measure the financial statement items as if the new policy had always been applied. (5)

Adjust the amounts of all prior periods presented (back to the opening balance sheet of the earliest period presented).

Exception

In some circumstances it is impracticable to adjust comparative information for one or more periods, for example because data is not (or is no longer) available. (50–53)

Adjust the amounts from the first period for which retrospective application is practicable.

Prospective application

Prospective application means that the changes in accounting policies cannot be made retrospectively, i.e. prior-period amounts are not adjusted. (5)

Instead, the new policies are applied from the beginning of the period in which the policy changed. The effect of the change is only recognised in the current and any future periods affected by the change.

KPMG

IAS 10 Events after the Reporting Period
(amended 2007)

Scope:	Accounting for and disclosure of events after the reporting period
Scope exclusions:	–
Core principles:	Events after the reporting period are those events that occur between the end of the reporting period and the date when the financial statements are authorised for issue. 'Adjusting events' are those that provide evidence of conditions that existed at the end of the reporting period. 'Non-adjusting events' are those that are indicative of conditions that arose after the reporting period. Such events are only disclosed in the notes, and include resolutions that are required to authorise dividend payments.
	Dividend payments that are authorised only after the reporting period are not recognised as a liability at the period end.
Effective date:	Annual periods beginning on or after 1 January 2005. Earlier application is encouraged.
Applies to:	All entities

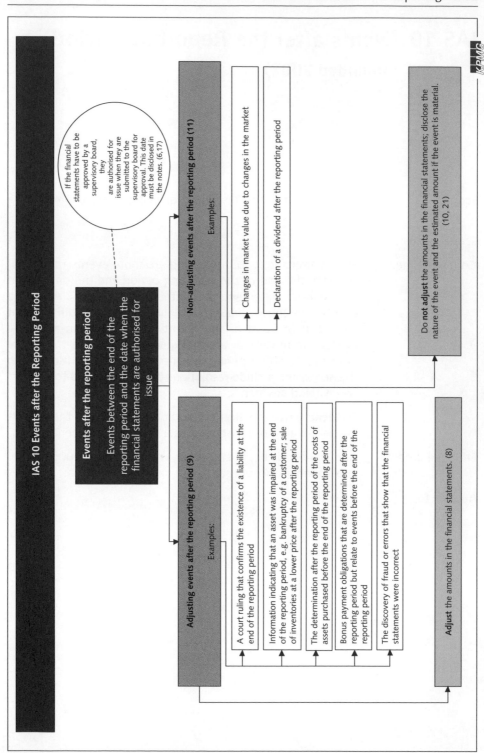

IAS 10 Events after the Reporting Period

Events after the reporting period

Events between the end of the reporting period and the date when the financial statements are authorised for issue

If the financial statements have to be approved by a supervisory board, they are authorised for issue when they are submitted to the supervisory board for approval. This date must be disclosed in the notes. (6,17)

Adjusting events after the reporting period (9)

Examples:

A court ruling that confirms the existence of a liability at the end of the reporting period

Information indicating that an asset was impaired at the end of the reporting period, e.g. bankruptcy of a customer; sale of inventories at a lower price after the reporting period

The determination after the reporting period of the costs of assets purchased before the end of the reporting period

Bonus payment obligations that are determined after the reporting period but relate to events before the end of the reporting period

The discovery of fraud or errors that show that the financial statements were incorrect

Adjust the amounts in the financial statements. (8)

Non-adjusting events after the reporting period (11)

Examples:

Changes in market value due to changes in the market

Declaration of a dividend after the reporting period

Do **not adjust** the amounts in the financial statements; disclose the nature of the event and the estimated amount if the event is material. (10, 21)

KPMG

IAS 11 Construction Contracts
(amended 2007)

Scope: Accounting for construction contracts

Scope exclusions: –

Core principles: Construction contracts are contracts specifically negotiated for the construction of assets that are usually completed over several reporting periods. In contrast to other contracts, costs and revenues are not recognised when the risks and rewards under the contract are transferred. Provided that certain criteria are met, they are recognised during the course of the contract by reference to the stage of completion – in other words, part of the profit is recognised before completion ('percentage of completion' method). The stage of completion can be determined using three different methods.

The requirements for fixed price contracts are stricter than those for cost plus contracts.

Any forecast losses on construction contracts must be recognised immediately in full as an expense.

Effective date: Annual periods beginning on or after 1 January 1995.

Applies to: All entities

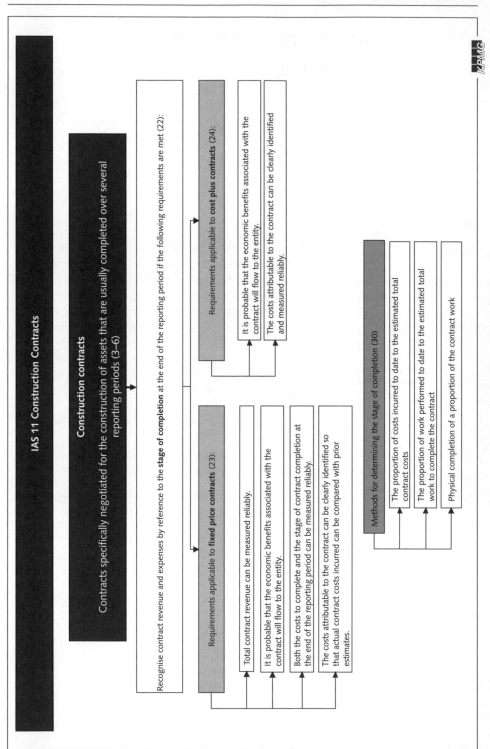

IAS 11 Construction Contracts

Construction contracts

Contracts specifically negotiated for the construction of assets that are usually completed over several reporting periods (3–6)

Recognise contract revenue and expenses by reference to the **stage of completion** at the end of the reporting period if the following requirements are met (22):

Requirements applicable to **fixed price contracts** (23):

- Total contract revenue can be measured reliably.
- It is probable that the economic benefits associated with the contract will flow to the entity.
- Both the costs to complete and the stage of contract completion at the end of the reporting period can be measured reliably.
- The costs attributable to the contract can be clearly identified so that actual contract costs incurred can be compared with prior estimates.

Requirements applicable to **cost plus contracts** (24):

- It is probable that the economic benefits associated with the contract will flow to the entity.
- The costs attributable to the contract can be clearly identified and measured reliably.

Methods for determining the stage of completion (30)

- The proportion of costs incurred to date to the estimated total contract costs
- The proportion of work performed to date to the estimated total work to complete the contract
- Physical completion of a proportion of the contract work

IAS 12 Income Taxes (amended 2008)

Scope:	Accounting for income taxes
Scope exclusions:	Accounting for government grants or investment tax credits
Core principles:	Current tax is accounted for in the period in which the taxable profit or losses that give rise to the tax occur.

Deferred income tax is accounted for using the 'balance sheet liability method', under which deferred taxes are recognised for all temporary differences between the carrying amount of assets and liabilities in the IFRS statement of financial position and their tax base. Temporary differences are differences that result in taxable (taxable temporary differences) or deductible (deductible temporary differences) amounts when the carrying amount of an asset is recovered or the carrying amount of a liability is settled. Taxable temporary differences lead to the recognition of a deferred tax liability, while deductible temporary differences lead to the recognition of deferred tax assets. Exceptions to this principle include certain differences relating to goodwill, as well as the initial recognition of an asset or a liability in a transaction that is not a business combination and does not affect profit or loss. In addition, deferred tax assets are recognised for unused tax loss carryforwards and tax credits to the extent that it is probable that future taxable profit will be available.

Deferred tax assets and liabilities are measured at the tax rates that are expected to apply to the period when the asset is realised or the liability is settled. Deferred taxes may not be discounted, irrespective of their maturity. The carrying amounts of deferred tax assets must be written down to the extent that it is no longer probable that sufficient taxable profit will be available to allow them to be utilised.

Effective date:	Annual periods beginning on or after 1 January 1998. Amendments resulting from IAS 1 (amended 2007) and IFRS 3 (amended 2008) must be applied at the same time as the amended IAS 1 and IFRS 3 respectively.
Applies to:	All entities

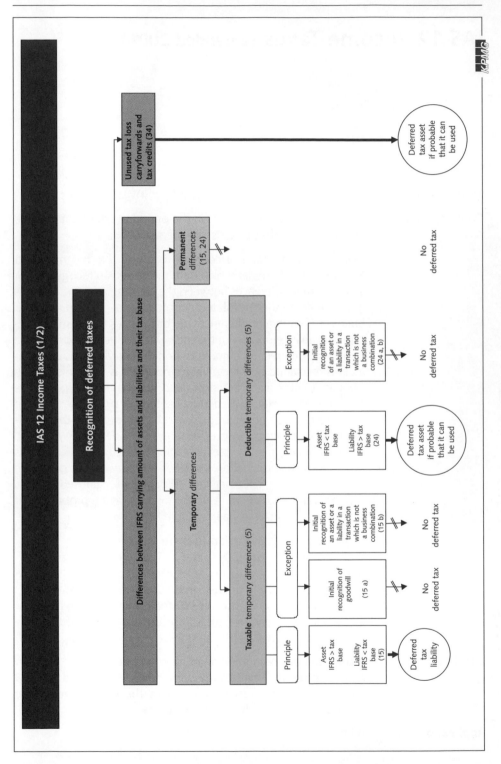

IAS 12 Income Taxes (1/2)

Recognition of deferred taxes

Differences between IFRS carrying amount of assets and liabilities and their tax base

Unused tax loss carryforwards and tax credits (34)

Deferred tax asset if probable that it can be used

Permanent differences (15, 24)

No deferred tax

Temporary differences

Taxable temporary differences (5)

Principle

Asset IFRS > tax base
Liability IFRS < tax base (15)

Deferred tax liability

Exception

Initial recognition of goodwill (15 a)

No deferred tax

Initial recognition of an asset or a liability in a transaction which is not a business combination (15 b)

No deferred tax

Deductible temporary differences (5)

Principle

Asset IFRS < tax base
Liability IFRS > tax base (24)

Deferred tax asset if probable that it can be used

Exception

Initial recognition of an asset or a liability in a transaction which is not a business combination (24 a, b)

No deferred tax

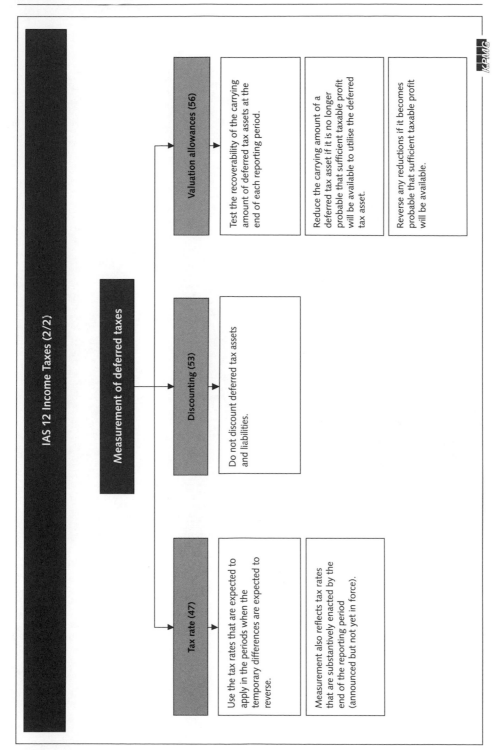

IAS 12 Income Taxes (2/2)

Measurement of deferred taxes

Tax rate (47)

Use the tax rates that are expected to apply in the periods when the temporary differences are expected to reverse.

Measurement also reflects tax rates that are substantively enacted by the end of the reporting period (announced but not yet in force).

Discounting (53)

Do not discount deferred tax assets and liabilities.

Valuation allowances (56)

Test the recoverability of the carrying amount of deferred tax assets at the end of each reporting period.

Reduce the carrying amount of a deferred tax asset if it is no longer probable that sufficient taxable profit will be available to utilise the deferred tax asset.

Reverse any reductions if it becomes probable that sufficient taxable profit will be available.

KPMG

IAS 14 Segment Reporting (amended 2007)

Scope:	Preparation and presentation of segment reporting
Scope exclusions:	–
Core principles:	Segment reporting is included in the notes to the financial statements and is divided into a primary and a secondary reporting format. The reportable segments are identified using a three-step approach. First, the entity must decide whether business or geographical segments are the primary reporting format. The other of the two is the secondary reporting format. In the next step, the entity's segments are identified using the 'management approach', if appropriate after adjustments to reflect risk and return considerations. Segments are only reportable if they meet certain materiality criteria.
	Ten disclosures are required for the primary reporting format, but only three for the secondary reporting format.
	Intra-segment transactions must be eliminated. The total segment amounts and the aggregated financial statement information must be reconciled.
	The main segment reporting disclosures include the pricing policy for inter-segment transfers and a description of the nature of the business and geographical segments.
Effective date:	Annual periods beginning on or after 1 July 1998. IAS 14 is being replaced by IFRS 8, which must be applied no later than for annual periods beginning on or after 1 January 2009.
Applies to:	Publicly traded entities only.

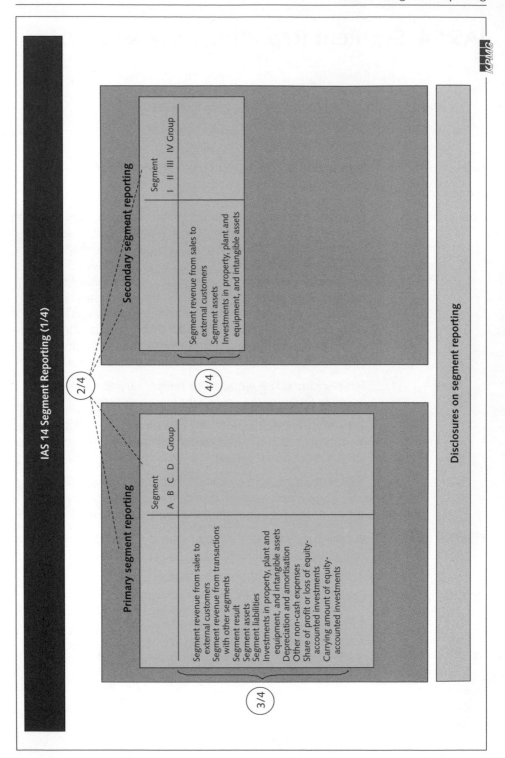

IAS 14 Segment Reporting (1/4)

Primary segment reporting

	Segment				
	A	B	C	D	Group
Segment revenue from sales to external customers					
Segment revenue from transactions with other segments					
Segment result					
Segment assets					
Segment liabilities					
Investments in property, plant and equipment, and intangible assets					
Depreciation and amortisation					
Other non-cash expenses					
Share of profit or loss of equity-accounted investments					
Carrying amount of equity-accounted investments					

3/4

2/4

Secondary segment reporting

	Segment				
	I	II	III	IV	Group
Segment revenue from sales to external customers					
Segment assets					
Investments in property, plant and equipment, and intangible assets					

4/4

Disclosures on segment reporting

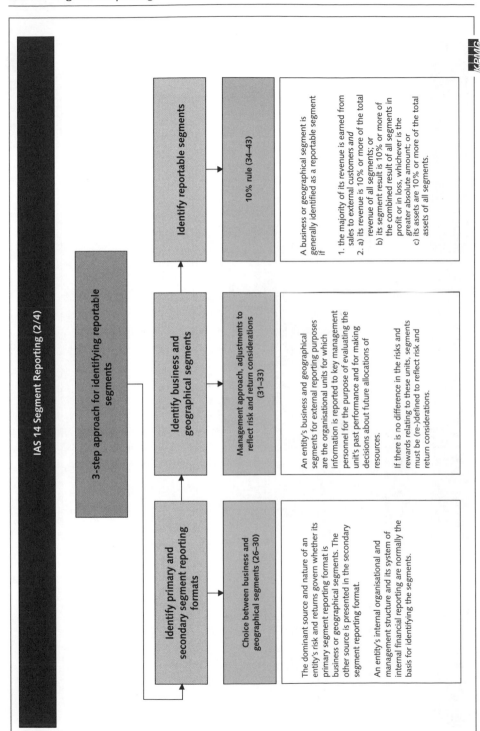

IAS 14 Segment Reporting (2/4)

3-step approach for identifying reportable segments

Identify primary and secondary segment reporting formats

Choice between business and geographical segments (26–30)

The dominant source and nature of an entity's risk and returns govern whether its primary segment reporting format is business or geographical segments. The other source is presented in the secondary segment reporting format.

An entity's internal organisational and management structure and its system of internal financial reporting are normally the basis for identifying the segments.

Identify business and geographical segments

Management approach, adjustments to reflect risk and return considerations (31–33)

An entity's business and geographical segments for external reporting purposes are the organisational units for which information is reported to key management personnel for the purpose of evaluating the unit's past performance and for making decisions about future allocations of resources.

If there is no difference in the risks and rewards relating to these units, segments must be (re-)defined to reflect risk and return considerations.

Identify reportable segments

10% rule (34–43)

A business or geographical segment is generally identified as a reportable segment if

1. the majority of its revenue is earned from sales to external customers *and*
2. a) its revenue is 10% or more of the total revenue of all segments; or
   b) its segment result is 10% or more of the combined result of all segments in profit or in loss, whichever is the greater absolute amount; or
   c) its assets are 10% or more of the total assets of all segments.

KPMG

IAS 14 Segment Reporting (3/4)

Disclosures on the primary reporting format

Revenue from sales to external customers (16, 51)	• All revenue reported in the income statement that is directly attributable to a segment or the relevant portion of revenue that can be allocated to the segment on a reasonable basis, except interest, dividend income and gains on sales of investments • Revenue from sales to external customers is earned from non-group entities
Revenue from other segments (51)	• Revenue from other segments is earned from other segments. • Intra-segment revenue is eliminated.
Segment result (16, 52)	• Segment revenue less segment expense • Segment expenses are expenses resulting from the operating activities of a segment that are directly attributable to the segment or the relevant portion of expenses that can be allocated to the segment on a reasonable basis, except interest, losses on sales of investments, share of loss of equity-accounted investments and income tax expense.
Segment assets (16, 55)	• Operating assets that are employed by a segment in its operating activities and that either are directly attributable to the segment or can be allocated to the segment on a reasonable basis. • In principle, may also include goodwill.
Segment liabilities (16, 56)	• All operating liabilities that result from the operating activities of a segment and that either are directly attributable to the segment or can be allocated to the segment on a reasonable basis, except income tax liabilities and interest-bearing borrowings.
Investments in property, plant and equipment, and intangible assets (57)	• On an accrual, not a cash basis.
Depreciation and amortisation (58)	• Depreciation and amortisation, plus impairment losses (disclose separately in accordance with IAS 36.129) • Not required if segment cash flows are disclosed on a voluntary basis.
Other non-cash expenses (61)	• Not required if segment cash flows are disclosed on a voluntary basis.
Share of profit or loss of equity-accounted investments (64)	• Share of profit or loss of equity-accounted associates or joint ventures if substantially all of those investees' operations are within a single segment.
Carrying amount of equity-accounted investments (66)	• Carrying amount of the entity's investments in equity-accounted associates and joint ventures.

KPMG

IAS 14 Segment Reporting (4/4)

Disclosure on the secondary reporting formats

Disclosures if the primary segment reporting format is business segments:

Additional disclosures required, depending on the presentation of geographical segments. (71, 72)

Revenue from sales to external customers (69 a)

- To the same extent as in the primary reporting format, based on the geographical location of customers

Segment assets (69 b)

- To the same extent as in the primary reporting format, based on the geographical location of assets

Investments in property, plant and equipment, and intangible assets (69 c)

- To the same extent as in the primary reporting format, based on the geographical location of assets

Disclosures if the primary segment reporting format is geographical segments:

Revenue from sales to external customers (70a)

- To the same extent as in the primary reporting format, by business segments

Segment assets (70b)

- To the same extent as in the primary reporting format, by business segments

Investments in property, plant and equipment, and intangible assets (70c)

- To the same extent as in the primary reporting format, by business segments

KPMG

IAS 16 Property, Plant and Equipment
(amended 2008)

Scope:	Accounting for property, plant and equipment
Scope exclusions:	Biological assets, mineral rights and similar resources
Core principles:	Items of property, plant and equipment are recognised as assets if it is probable that future economic benefits will flow to the entity and their cost can be measured reliably.
	Property, plant and equipment is initially measured at cost. Purchase cost comprises the purchase price, less purchase price reductions, plus other directly attributable costs. Together with direct labour and material costs, production cost includes production-related indirect costs, i.e. the same components as inventories in accordance with IAS 2. IAS 23 requires borrowing costs to be capitalised. Costs of dismantling an item and restoring the site are included in the cost of the asset, provided that they have to be recognised as provisions in accordance with IAS 37 and that they arise from the installation or use of the item for purposes other than for producing inventories.
	Subsequent measurement of each class of property, plant and equipment uses either the cost model or the revaluation model. Under the cost model, the asset is carried at cost less depreciation and less impairment losses/plus reversals of impairment losses in accordance with IAS 36. Under the revaluation model, items of property, plant and equipment are regularly revalued at their fair value. Increases in fair value are generally recognised in other comprehensive income, while decreases in fair value are generally recognised in profit or loss. The same procedure as for the cost model is applied between revaluation dates.
Effective date:	Annual periods beginning on or after 1 January 2005. Earlier application is encouraged. Amendments resulting from IAS 1 (amended 2007) and IFRS 3 (amended 2008) must be applied at the same time as the amended IAS 1 and IFRS 3 respectively.
Applies to:	All entities

IAS 16 Property, Plant and Equipment (1/3)

Initial measurement

Costs of purchase

Purchase price less purchase price reductions **(16 a)**

Other directly attributable costs, e.g.: (16 b)

- Costs of employee benefits
- Costs of site preparation
- Initial delivery and handling costs
- Installation and assembly costs
- Fees for architects, engineers

Borrowing costs in accordance with IAS 23

Costs of dismantling and removing an item and restoring the site are included in the cost of the asset provided that they must be recognised in accordance with IAS 37 and that they arise from the installation or use of the item for purposes other than for producing inventories. **(16 c)**

Do not include:

- Costs of opening a new facility (19 a)
- Costs of introducing a new product or service (19 b)
- Business relocation costs (including staff training costs) (19 c)
- Administration and other general overhead costs (19 d)

Costs of conversion (22)

- Direct material and labour costs
- Production-related indirect costs

as in **IAS 2**

Costs of exchange transactions

Measure at **fair value** if
- the exchange transaction has commercial substance and
- the fair value of either of the assets involved is reliably measurable. (24)

An exchange transaction has **commercial substance** if the configuration of the cash flows of the asset received differs from that of the cash flows of the asset transferred; or the entity-specific value of the portion of the entitys operation affected changes as a result of the exchange; and the difference is significant relative to the fair value of the asset exchanged. (25)

The fair value of an asset is **reliably measurable**, even if comparable market transactions do not exist, if the variability in the range of fair value estimates is not significant for that asset or the probabilities of the various estimates within the range can be reasonably assessed and used. (26)

If the fair values of both assets can be determined, the fair value of the asset given up is used to measure the cost of the asset received unless the fair value of the asset received is more clearly evident. (26)

KPMG

IAS 16 Property, Plant and Equipment (2/3)

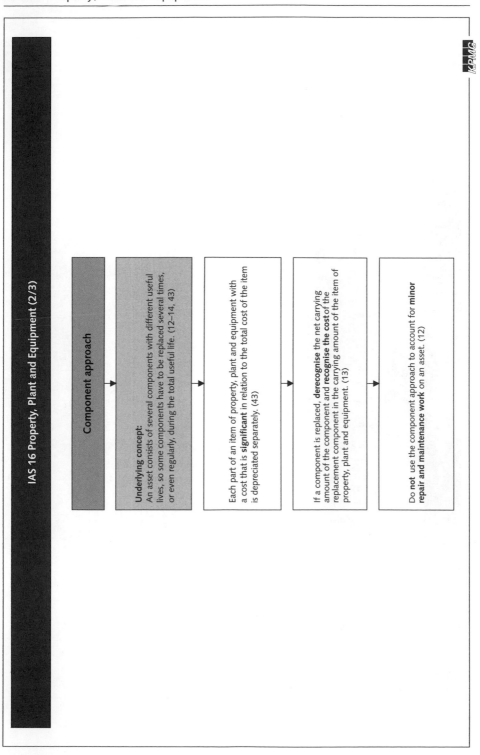

Component approach

Underlying concept:
An asset consists of several components with different useful lives, so some components have to be replaced several times, or even regularly, during the total useful life. (12–14, 43)

Each part of an item of property, plant and equipment with a cost that is **significant** in relation to the total cost of the item is depreciated separately. (43)

If a component is replaced, **derecognise** the net carrying amount of the component and **recognise the cost** of the replacement component in the carrying amount of the item of property, plant and equipment. (13)

Do **not** use the component approach to account for **minor repair and maintenance work** on an asset. (12)

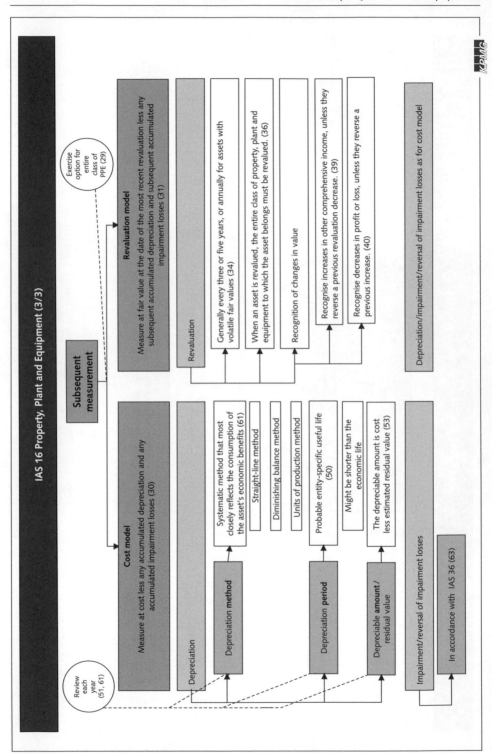

IAS 16 Property, Plant and Equipment (3/3)

Subsequent measurement

Review each year (51, 61)

Exercise option for entire class of PPE (29)

Cost model

Measure at cost less any accumulated depreciation and any accumulated impairment losses (30)

Depreciation

Depreciation method

- Systematic method that most closely reflects the consumption of the asset's economic benefits (61)
  - Straight-line method
  - Diminishing balance method
  - Units of production method

Depreciation period

- Probable entity-specific useful life (50)
- Might be shorter than the economic life

Depreciable amount / residual value

- The depreciable amount is cost less estimated residual value (53)

Impairment/reversal of impairment losses

In accordance with IAS 36 (63)

Revaluation model

Measure at fair value at the date of the most recent revaluation less any subsequent accumulated depreciation and subsequent accumulated impairment losses (31)

Revaluation

- Generally every three or five years, or annually for assets with volatile fair values (34)
- When an asset is revalued, the entire class of property, plant and equipment to which the asset belongs must be revalued. (36)
- Recognition of changes in value
  - Recognise increases in other comprehensive income, unless they reverse a previous revaluation decrease. (39)
  - Recognise decreases in profit or loss, unless they reverse a previous increase. (40)

Depreciation/impairment/reversal of impairment losses as for cost model

KPMG

IAS 17 Leases (amended 2005)

Scope: Accounting for leases

Scope exclusions: Leases to explore for or to use minerals, oil, natural gas and similar resources, and licensing agreements for films, patents and similar rights. Similarly, the standard cannot be applied as the basis of measurement for certain investment properties or biological assets.

Core principles: Leases are classified as finance leases if substantially all the risks and rewards transfer to the lessee. Otherwise they are classified as operating leases.

In a finance lease, the lessee is the beneficial owner and must recognise the asset. The asset is recognised at the lower of its fair value and the present value of the minimum lease payments. A liability is recognised in the same amount. The asset is depreciated or amortised over the shorter of the lease term and its useful life. The lease expenditure is divided between repayments of principal and finance charges. The lessor recognises a receivable. Lease payments received are divided between repayment of the principal and finance income.

The legal owner is also the beneficial owner in operating leases.

Effective date: Annual periods beginning on or after 1 January 2005. Earlier application is encouraged.

Applies to: All entities

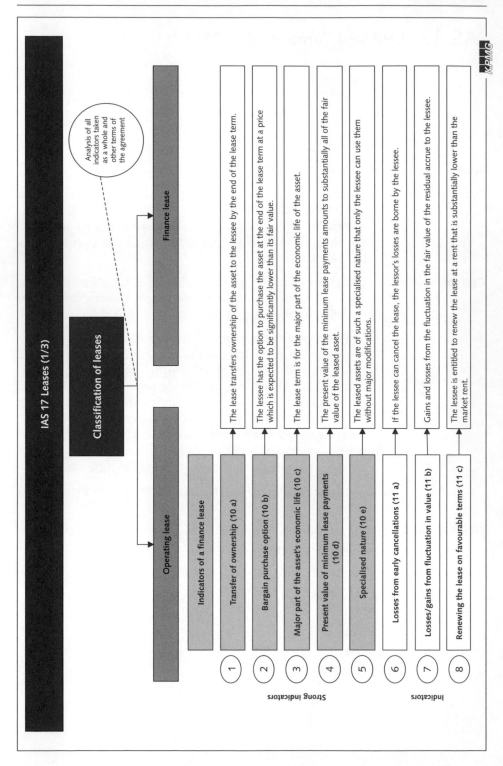

IAS 17 Leases (1/3)

Classification of leases

Analysis of all indicators taken as a whole and other terms of the agreement

Operating lease

Finance lease

Strong Indicators

Indicators of a finance lease

1 Transfer of ownership (10 a)
The lease transfers ownership of the asset to the lessee by the end of the lease term.

2 Bargain purchase option (10 b)
The lessee has the option to purchase the asset at the end of the lease term at a price which is expected to be significantly lower than its fair value.

3 Major part of the asset's economic life (10 c)
The lease term is for the major part of the economic life of the asset.

4 Present value of minimum lease payments (10 d)
The present value of the minimum lease payments amounts to substantially all of the fair value of the leased asset.

5 Specialised nature (10 e)
The leased assets are of such a specialised nature that only the lessee can use them without major modifications.

Indicators

6 Losses from early cancellations (11 a)
If the lessee can cancel the lease, the lessor's losses are borne by the lessee.

7 Losses/gains from fluctuation in value (11 b)
Gains and losses from the fluctuation in the fair value of the residual accrue to the lessee.

8 Renewing the lease on favourable terms (11 c)
The lessee is entitled to renew the lease at a rent that is substantially lower than the market rent.

KPMG

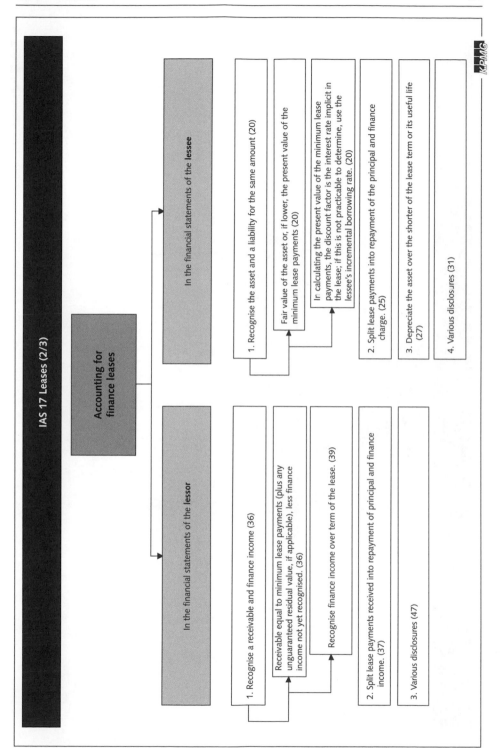

IAS 17 Leases (2/3)

Accounting for finance leases

In the financial statements of the **lessee**

1. Recognise the asset and a liability for the same amount (20)

Fair value of the asset or, if lower, the present value of the minimum lease payments (20)

In calculating the present value of the minimum lease payments, the discount factor is the interest rate implicit in the lease; if this is not practicable to determine, use the lessee's incremental borrowing rate. (20)

2. Split lease payments into repayment of the principal and finance charge. (25)

3. Depreciate the asset over the shorter of the lease term or its useful life (27)

4. Various disclosures (31)

In the financial statements of the **lessor**

1. Recognise a receivable and finance income (36)

Receivable equal to minimum lease payments (plus any unguaranteed residual value, if applicable), less finance income not yet recognised. (36)

Recognise finance income over term of the lease. (39)

2. Split lease payments received into repayment of principal and finance income. (37)

3. Various disclosures (47)

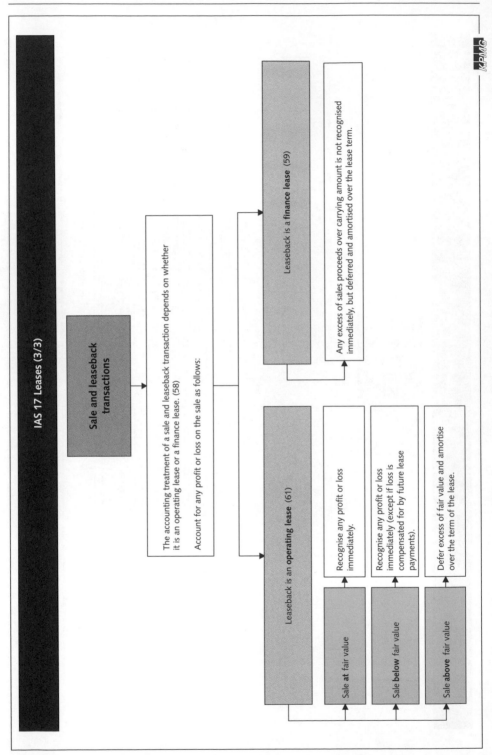

IAS 17 Leases (3/3)

Sale and leaseback transactions

The accounting treatment of a sale and leaseback transaction depends on whether it is an operating lease or a finance lease. (58)

Account for any profit or loss on the sale as follows:

Leaseback is a finance lease (59)

Any excess of sales proceeds over carrying amount is not recognised immediately, but deferred and amortised over the lease term.

Leaseback is an operating lease (61)

Sale **at** fair value — Recognise any profit or loss immediately.

Sale **below** fair value — Recognise any profit or loss immediately (except if loss is compensated for by future lease payments).

Sale **above** fair value — Defer excess of fair value and amortise over the term of the lease.

KPMG

IAS 18 Revenue (amended 2004)

Scope:	Accounting for revenue
Scope exclusions:	Revenue from leases; dividends from investments that are accounted for using the equity method; insurance contracts; changes in the fair value of financial instruments in accordance with IAS 39; changes in the value of other current assets; initial recognition and changes in the fair value of biological assets; initial recognition of agricultural produce; extraction of mineral ores.
Core principles:	General requirements for revenue recognition are that the amount can be measured reliably and that it is probable that the economic benefits from the transaction will flow to the entity. Additional special requirements apply to the following categories: sale of goods, rendering of services, interest, royalties and dividends.
	Revenue is measured at the fair value of the consideration received or receivable.
Effective date:	Annual periods beginning on or after 1 January 1995.
Applies to:	All entities

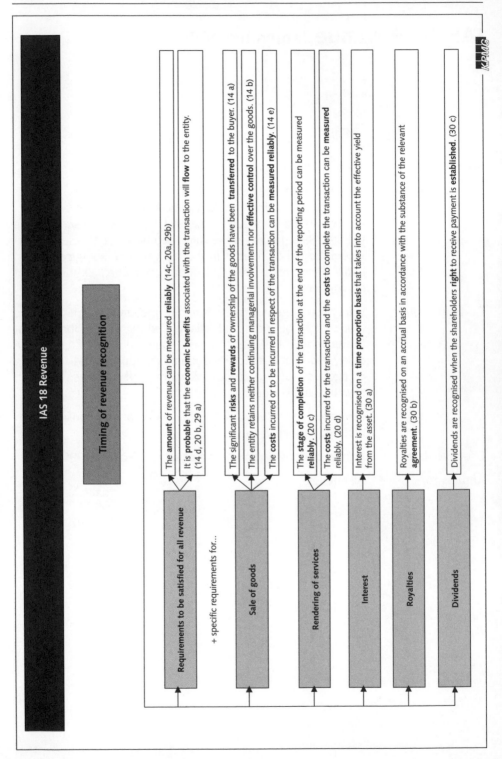

IAS 18 Revenue

Timing of revenue recognition

Requirements to be satisfied for all revenue

The **amount** of revenue can be measured **reliably**. (14c, 20a, 29b)

It is **probable** that the **economic benefits** associated with the transaction will **flow** to the entity. (14 d, 20 b, 29 a)

+ specific requirements for...

Sale of goods

The significant **risks** and **rewards** of ownership of the goods have been **transferred** to the buyer. (14 a)

The entity retains neither continuing managerial involvement nor **effective control** over the goods. (14 b)

The **costs** incurred or to be incurred in respect of the transaction can be **measured reliably**. (14 e)

Rendering of services

The **stage of completion** of the transaction at the end of the reporting period can be measured **reliably**. (20 c)

The **costs** incurred for the transaction and the **costs** to complete the transaction can be **measured** reliably. (20 d)

Interest

Interest is recognised on a **time proportion basis** that takes into account the effective yield from the asset. (30 a)

Royalties

Royalties are recognised on an accrual basis in accordance with the substance of the relevant **agreement**. (30 b)

Dividends

Dividends are recognised when the shareholders **right** to receive payment is **established**. (30 c)

IAS 19 Employee Benefits (amended 2007)

Scope: Accounting for employee benefits

Scope exclusions: Share-based payments within the scope of IFRS 2

Core principles: Accounting for employee benefits primarily depends on their classification as short-term employee benefits, post-employment benefits, other long-term employee benefits, or termination benefits.

'Post-employment benefits' are the most complex category. Depending on the type of pension plan (defined contribution plan or defined benefit plan), the expense recognised for the period is either the entity's contribution payable in the period or the amount transferred to a pension provision.

To calculate the pension provisions, the future defined benefit obligations are discounted using an interest rate corresponding to the yield on bonds of a similar duration. Measurement of the obligations reflects future salary increases. Three different methods may be used to recognise actuarial gains or losses resulting from changes in the parameters over time.

Effective date: Essentially for annual periods beginning on or after 1 January 1999. Certain paragraphs have later effective dates. Amendments resulting from IAS 1 (amended 2007) must be applied at the same time as the amended IAS 1.

Applies to: All entities

IAS 19 Employee Benefits (1/5)

Classification of employee benefits

Short-term employee benefits (8–23)

- **Wages, salaries and social security contributions**
- Short-term **compensated absences**
- **Profit-sharing and bonuses** payable within 12 months after end of period in which the employees rendered the related service
- **Non-monetary benefits** (such as company cars, medical care) for current employees

Expense/ liability in the reporting period, no discounting

Post-employment benefits (24–125)

- **Retirement benefits**, such as pensions
- **Other post-employment benefits**, such as life insurance and medical care

2/5

Other long-term employee benefits (126–131)

Examples:
- **Long-term compensated absences**
- Jubilee benefits
- Long-term **disability benefits**
- **Profit-sharing and bonuses (not share-based)** payable 12 months or more after end of period in which the employees rendered the related service
- **Deferred compensation** paid 12 months or more after end of period in which it was earned

Expense/ liability; present value of DBO less fair value of plan assets

---

Termination benefits (132–143)

The entity is **demonstrably committed** to either
a) terminating the employment of an employee before the normal retirement date; or
b) providing termination benefits as a result of the employee's acceptance of an offer made to encourage voluntary redundancy.

Commitment requires a **detailed formal plan**, incl.
- Location, function, approx. number of employees
- Termination benefits
- Timing of implementation

Expense only if demonstrable commitment; discounted if >12 months

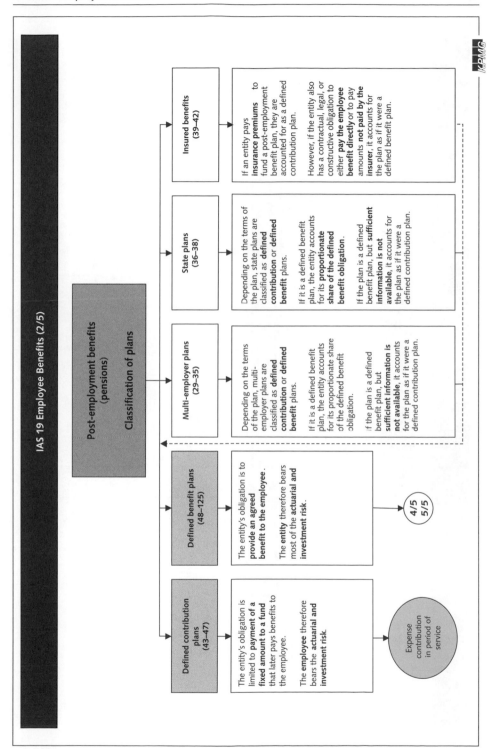

IAS 19 Employee Benefits (2/5)

Post-employment benefits (pensions)

Classification of plans

Defined contribution plans (43–47)

The entity's obligation is limited to **payment of a fixed amount to a fund** that later pays benefits to the employee.

The **employee** therefore bears the **actuarial and investment risk**.

Expense contribution in period of service

Defined benefit plans (48–125)

The entity's obligation is to **provide an agreed benefit to the employee**.

The **entity** therefore bears most of the **actuarial and investment risk**.

4/5
5/5

Multi-employer plans (29–35)

Depending on the terms of the plan, multi-employer plans are classified as **defined contribution** or **defined benefit** plans.

If it is a defined benefit plan, the entity accounts for its proportionate share of the defined benefit obligation.

If the plan is a defined benefit plan, but **sufficient information is not available**, it accounts for the plan as if it were a defined contribution plan.

State plans (36–38)

Depending on the terms of the plan, state plans are classified as **defined contribution** or **defined benefit** plans.

If it is a defined benefit plan, the entity accounts for its **proportionate share of the defined benefit obligation**.

If the plan is a defined benefit plan, but **sufficient information is not available**, it accounts for the plan as if it were a defined contribution plan.

Insured benefits (39–42)

If an entity pays **insurance premiums** to fund a post-employment benefit plan, they are accounted for as a defined contribution plan.

However, if the entity also has a contractual, legal, or constructive obligation to either **pay the employee benefit directly** or to pay amounts **not paid by the insurer**, it accounts for the plan as if it were a defined benefit plan.

KPMG

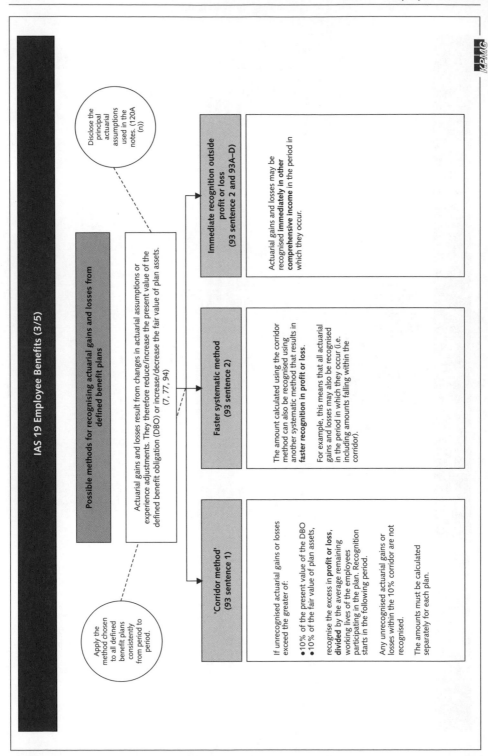

IAS 19 Employee Benefits (3/5)

Disclose the principal actuarial assumptions used in the notes. (120A (n))

Apply the method chosen to all defined benefit plans consistently from period to period.

Possible methods for recognising actuarial gains and losses from defined benefit plans

Actuarial gains and losses result from changes in actuarial assumptions or experience adjustments. They therefore reduce/increase the present value of the defined benefit obligation (DBO) or increase/decrease the fair value of plan assets. (7, 77, 94)

'Corridor method' (93 sentence 1)

If unrecognised actuarial gains or losses exceed the greater of:

- 10% of the present value of the DBO
- 10% of the fair value of plan assets,

recognise the excess in **profit or loss**, **divided** by the average remaining working lives of the employees participating in the plan. Recognition starts in the following period.

Any unrecognised actuarial gains or losses within the 10% corridor are not recognised.

The amounts must be calculated separately for each plan.

Faster systematic method (93 sentence 2)

The amount calculated using the corridor method can also be recognised using another systematic method that results in **faster recognition in profit or loss.**

For example, this means that all actuarial gains and losses may also be recognised in the period in which they occur (i.e. including amounts falling within the corridor).

Immediate recognition outside profit or loss (93 sentence 2 and 93A–D)

Actuarial gains and losses may be recognised **immediately in other comprehensive income** in the period in which they occur.

KPMG

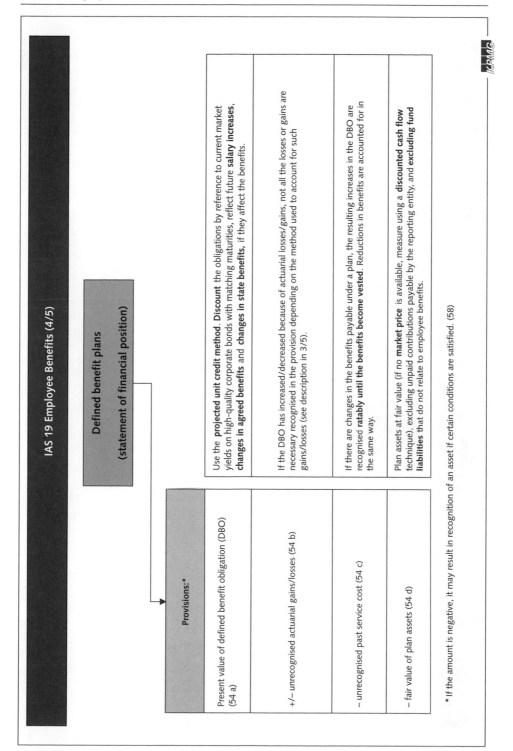

IAS 19 Employee Benefits (4/5)

Defined benefit plans

(statement of financial position)

Provisions:*

Present value of defined benefit obligation (DBO) (54 a)	Use the **projected unit credit method**. **Discount** the obligations by reference to current market yields on high-quality corporate bonds with matching maturities, reflect future **salary increases, changes in agreed benefits** and **changes in state benefits**, if they affect the benefits.
+/– unrecognised actuarial gains/losses (54 b)	If the DBO has increased/decreased because of actuarial losses/gains, not all the losses or gains are necessary recognised in the provision depending on the method used to account for such gains/losses (see description in 3/5).
– unrecognised past service cost (54 c)	If there are changes in the benefits payable under a plan, the resulting increases in the DBO are recognised **ratably until the benefits become vested**. Reductions in benefits are accounted for in the same way.
– fair value of plan assets (54 d)	Plan assets at fair value (if no **market price** is available, measure using a **discounted cash flow** technique), excluding unpaid contributions payable by the reporting entity, and **excluding fund liabilities** that do not relate to employee benefits.

* If the amount is negative, it may result in recognition of an asset if certain conditions are satisfied. (58)

IAS 19 Employee Benefits (5/5)

Defined benefit plans

(profit or loss/statement of comprehensive income)

Expense:	
Current service cost (61 a)	Difference between the present values of the DBO at the beginning and end of the period, less actuarial losses, interest cost and past service cost, plus actuarial gains.
+ interest cost (61 b)	Interest cost is the present value of the DBO throughout the period, multiplied by the discount rate at the start of the period. Option to present as operating expense or interest expense, disclose in the notes.
− expected return on plan assets (61 c)	The difference between the expected and actual return on plan assets is an actuarial gain or loss.
+/− recognised actuarial gains and losses (61 d)	See description in 4/5.
+ recognised past service cost (61 e)	See description in 4/5.
+/− effect of any curtailments or settlements (61 f)	Recognise the effects of any curtailments or settlements immediately.

IAS 20 Accounting for Government Grants and Disclosure of Government Assistance (amended 2007)

Scope:	Accounting for and disclosure of government grants and other forms of government assistance
Scope exclusions:	Government participation in the ownership of the entity, government grants covered by IAS 41.
Core principles:	Government grants are transfers of resources by the government to an entity in return for past or future compliance with certain conditions relating to the entity's operating activities. Government grants are recognised when there is reasonable assurance that the entity will comply with the conditions attaching to them and the grants will be received. Government grants related to assets are presented in the statement of financial position either by deducting the grant from the carrying amount of the asset or by recognising it as deferred income. Grants related to income are either recognised as other income or deducted from the related expense.
	Government assistance that is provided unconditionally is recognised immediately.
Effective date:	Annual periods beginning on or after 1 January 1984. Amendments resulting from IAS 1 (amended 2007) must be applied at the same time as the amended IAS 1.
Applies to:	All entities

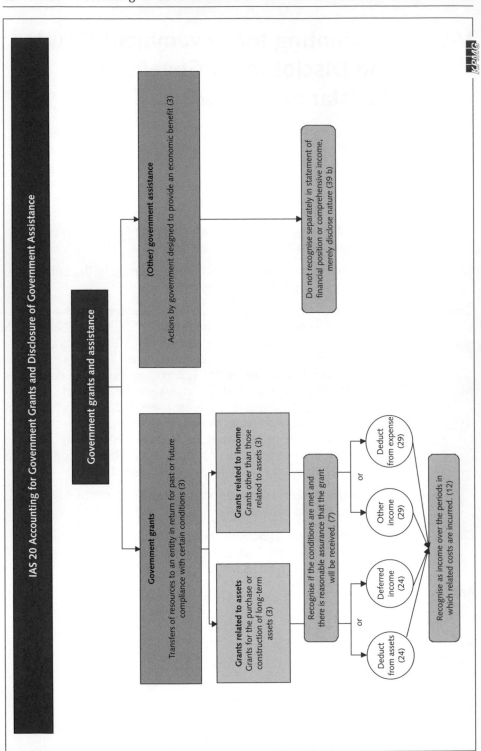

IAS 21 The Effects of Changes in Foreign Exchange Rates (amended 2008)

Scope:	Translation of transactions and balances in foreign currencies and translation of the financial statements of a foreign operation into a presentation currency
Scope exclusions:	Currency derivatives within the scope of IAS 39
Core principles:	An entity's functional currency is the currency of the primary economic environment in which it operates.
	Foreign currency transactions are translated into the functional currency of the reporting entity at the exchange rate at the date of transaction. At the end of the reporting period, monetary items are translated at the closing rate. Non-monetary items measured at historical cost continue to be translated at the rate at the transaction date. Non-monetary items measured using the revaluation model are translated at the date of the revaluation. Differences arising from these transactions are generally recognised in profit or loss or using the recognition method applied to gains/losses from revaluation.
	The financial statements of an entity included in the consolidated financial statements are translated into the group's presentation currency as follows. Assets and liabilities are translated at the closing rate, income and expenses at the rate at the transaction date (or average rates for simplification purposes). Goodwill and fair value adjustments from acquisition accounting are accounted for in the functional currency of the subsidiary and then translated into the presentation currency at the end of the reporting period. All exchange differences are recognised in other comprehensive income.
Effective date:	Annual periods beginning on or after 1 January 2005. Earlier application is encouraged. Amendments resulting from IAS 1 (amended 2007) and IAS 27 (amended 2008) must be applied at the same time as the amended IAS 1 and IAS 27 respectively.
Applies to:	All entities

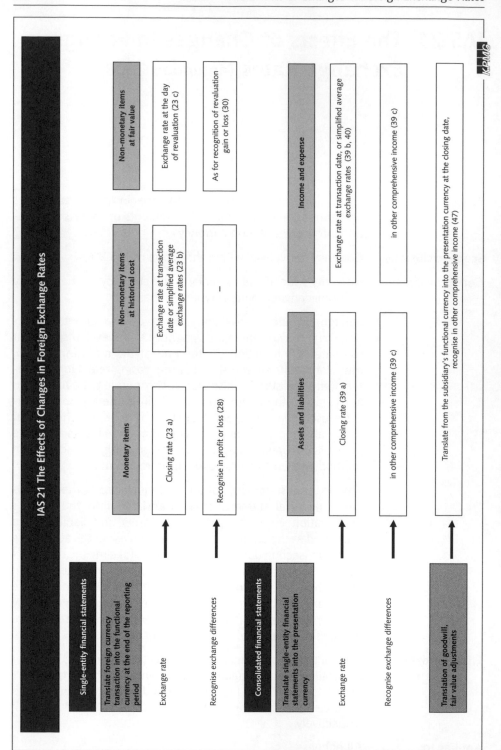

IAS 21 The Effects of Changes in Foreign Exchange Rates

Single-entity financial statements

Translate foreign currency transaction into the functional currency at the end of the reporting period

	Monetary items	Non-monetary items at historical cost	Non-monetary items at fair value
Exchange rate	Closing rate (23 a)	Exchange rate at transaction date or simplified average exchange rates (23 b)	Exchange rate at the day of revaluation (23 c)
Recognise exchange differences	Recognise in profit or loss (28)	–	As for recognition of revaluation gain or loss (30)

Consolidated financial statements

Translate single-entity financial statements into the presentation currency

	Assets and liabilities	Income and expense
Exchange rate	Closing rate (39 a)	Exchange rate at transaction date, or simplified average exchange rates (39 b, 40)
Recognise exchange differences	in other comprehensive income (39 c)	in other comprehensive income (39 c)

Translation of goodwill, fair value adjustments

Translate from the subsidiary's functional currency into the presentation currency at the closing date, recognise in other comprehensive income (47)

IAS 23 Borrowing Costs (amended 2007)

Scope:	Accounting for borrowing costs
Scope exclusions:	–
Core principles:	Borrowing costs are interest and other costs that an entity incurs in connection with the borrowing of funds.
	Borrowing costs that are directly attributable to the acquisition, construction, or production of a qualifying asset form part of the cost of that asset. Other borrowing costs are recognised as an expense.
	A qualifying asset is a non-financial asset that necessarily takes a substantial period of time to get ready for its intended use or sale. Assets that are routinely manufactured or otherwise produced in large quantities on a repetitive basis over a short period of time are not qualifying assets.
	If funds are borrowed specifically for the purpose of acquiring or producing a qualifying asset, the borrowing costs that are capitalised are the actual borrowing costs incurred during the period. If funds are borrowed generally, an average capitalisation rate of the financial liabilities used during the period that are not attributable to a specific asset is applied.
Effective date:	Qualifying assets recognised on or after 1 January 2009. IAS 23 (amended 2003) must be used until this date.
Applies to:	All entities

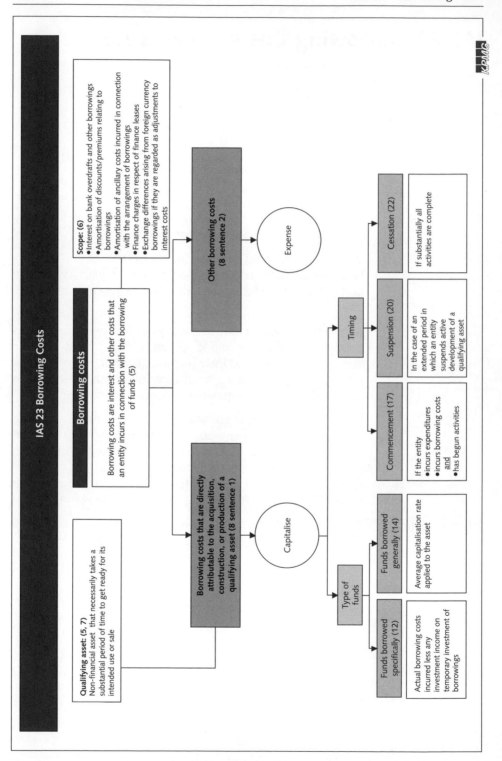

IAS 23 Borrowing Costs

Borrowing costs

Borrowing costs are interest and other costs that an entity incurs in connection with the borrowing of funds (5)

Scope: (6)
- Interest on bank overdrafts and other borrowings
- Amortisation of discounts/premiums relating to borrowings
- Amortisation of ancillary costs incurred in connection with the arrangement of borrowings
- Finance charges in respect of finance leases
- Exchange differences arising from foreign currency borrowings if they are regarded as adjustments to interest costs

Qualifying asset: (5, 7)
Non-financial asset that necessarily takes a substantial period of time to get ready for its intended use or sale

Other borrowing costs (8 sentence 2)

Expense

Borrowing costs that are directly attributable to the acquisition, construction, or production of a qualifying asset (8 sentence 1)

Capitalise

Timing

Cessation (22)

If substantially all activities are complete

Suspension (20)

In the case of an extended period in which an entity suspends active development of a qualifying asset

Commencement (17)

If the entity
- incurs expenditures
- incurs borrowing costs <u>and</u>
- has begun activities

Type of funds

Funds borrowed generally (14)

Average capitalisation rate applied to the asset

Funds borrowed specifically (12)

Actual borrowing costs incurred less any investment income on temporary investment of borrowings

KPMG

IAS 24 Related Party Disclosures
(amended 2007)

Scope: Identifying relationships and transactions with related parties, and determining the disclosures in the notes to be made about these items

Scope exclusions: –

Core principles: Related party relationships may exist with entities or natural persons who influence or are influenced by the reporting entity, with key management personnel and their close family members, and with post-employment benefit plans.

If there have been any transactions with these related parties, disclosures are required on the nature of the transactions, the amounts of the transactions and the amounts of outstanding balances, as well as their terms and conditions. The related party relationship must also be disclosed when control exists, even if there have been no transactions. The compensation of key management personnel compensation is disclosed in detail for each of five categories.

Effective date: Annual periods beginning on or after 1 January 2005. Earlier application is encouraged.

Applies to: All entities

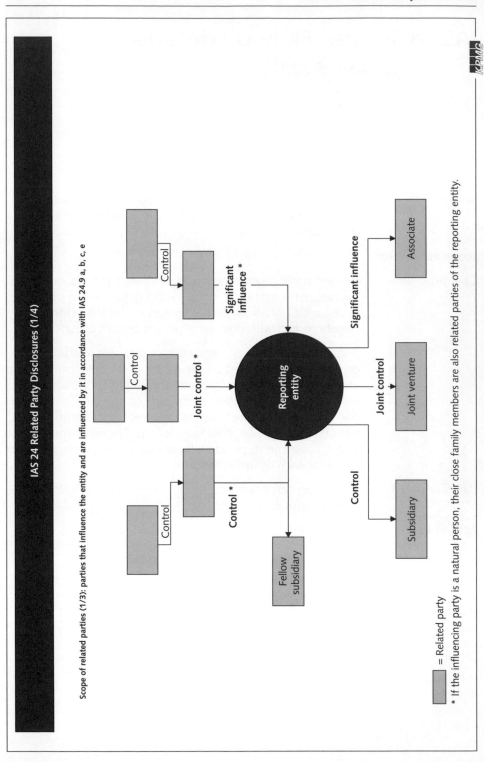

IAS 24 Related Party Disclosures (1/4)

Scope of related parties (1/3): parties that influence the entity and are influenced by it in accordance with IAS 24.9 a, b, c, e

Control

Control

Joint control *

Control

Control *

Significant influence *

Reporting entity

Fellow subsidiary

Significant influence

Joint control

Control

Associate

Joint venture

Subsidiary

= Related party

* If the influencing party is a natural person, their close family members are also related parties of the reporting entity.

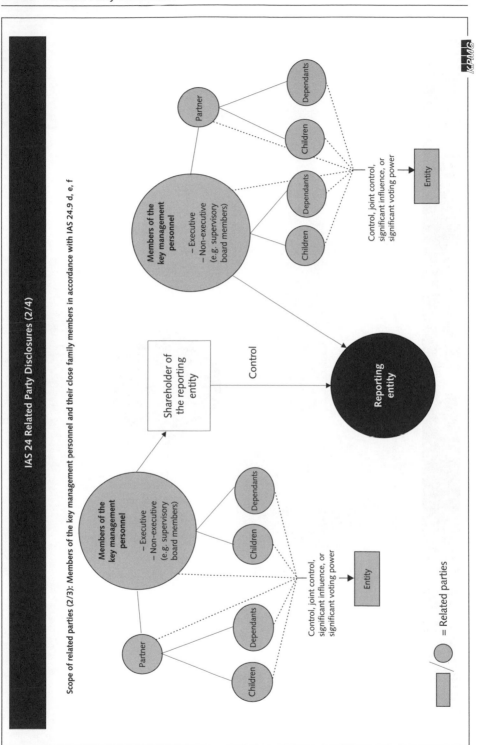

IAS 24 Related Party Disclosures (2/4)

Scope of related parties (2/3): Members of the key management personnel and their close family members in accordance with IAS 24.9 d, e, f

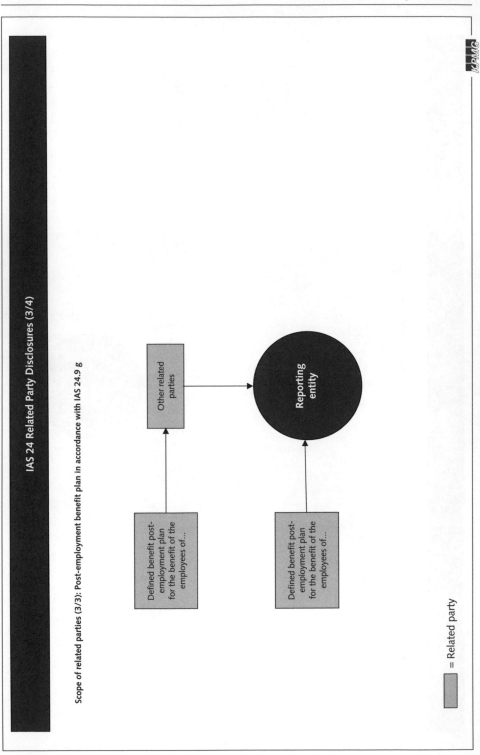

IAS 24 Related Party Disclosures (3/4)

Scope of related parties (3/3): Post-employment benefit plan in accordance with IAS 24.9 g

Other related parties

Reporting entity

Defined benefit post-employment plan for the benefit of the employees of...

Defined benefit post-employment plan for the benefit of the employees of...

= Related party

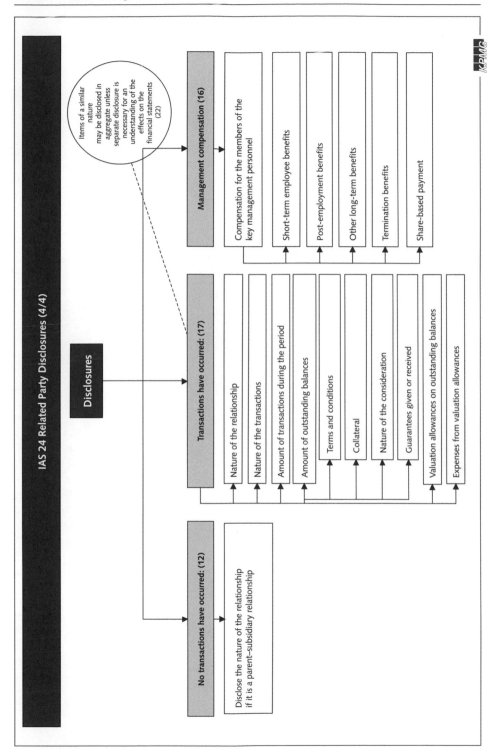

IAS 24 Related Party Disclosures (4/4)

Disclosures

Items of a similar nature may be disclosed in aggregate unless separate disclosure is necessary for an understanding of the effects on the financial statements (22)

No transactions have occurred: (12)

Disclose the nature of the relationship if it is a parent–subsidiary relationship

Transactions have occurred: (17)

Nature of the relationship

Nature of the transactions

Amount of transactions during the period

Amount of outstanding balances

Terms and conditions

Collateral

Nature of the consideration

Guarantees given or received

Valuation allowances on outstanding balances

Expenses from valuation allowances

Management compensation (16)

Compensation for the members of the key management personnel

Short-term employee benefits

Post-employment benefits

Other long-term benefits

Termination benefits

Share-based payment

KPMG

IAS 27 Consolidated and Separate Financial Statements (amended 2008)

Scope:	Preparation and presentation of consolidated financial statements, and accounting for investments in subsidiaries, jointly controlled entities and associates
Scope exclusions:	Methods of accounting for business combinations, including goodwill arising on a business combination
Core principles:	An entity must prepare consolidated financial statements if it has at least one subsidiary. In certain circumstances, an entity that is a sub-group parent may be exempt from the requirement to prepare consolidated financial statements.
	Subsidiaries are entities that are controlled by another entity. Control is the power to govern the financial and operating policies of an entity so as to obtain benefits from its activities.
	The assets, liabilities and equity of a subsidiary are included in full in the consolidated financial statements. Certain consolidation adjustments are then made. The carrying amount of the parent's investment in the subsidiary and the parent's portion of the equity of the subsidiary are eliminated. Intragroup transactions and balances are eliminated (elimination of intercompany profits, consolidation of intercompany balances, consolidation of income and expense). Non-controlling interests are presented separately within equity. Separate guidance covers consolidation after control is obtained, loss of control and other changes in the parent's ownership interest in the subsidiary.
Effective date:	Annual periods beginning on or after 1 January 2005. Amendments to IAS 27 made in 2008 must be applied for annual periods beginning on or after 1 July 2009; earlier application is permitted, provided that IFRS 3 (2008) is applied at the same time.
Applies to:	All entities

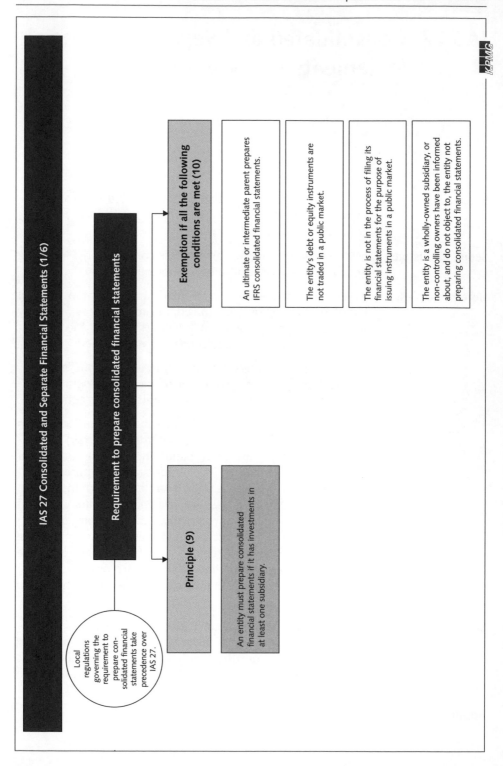

IAS 27 Consolidated and Separate Financial Statements (1/6)

Requirement to prepare consolidated financial statements

Local regulations governing the requirement to prepare consolidated financial statements take precedence over IAS 27.

Principle (9)

An entity must prepare consolidated financial statements if it has investments in at least one subsidiary.

Exemption if all the following conditions are met (10)

An ultimate or intermediate parent prepares IFRS consolidated financial statements.

The entity's debt or equity instruments are not traded in a public market.

The entity is not in the process of filing its financial statements for the purpose of issuing instruments in a public market.

The entity is a wholly-owned subsidiary, or non-controlling owners have been informed about, and do not object to, the entity not preparing consolidated financial statements.

KPMG

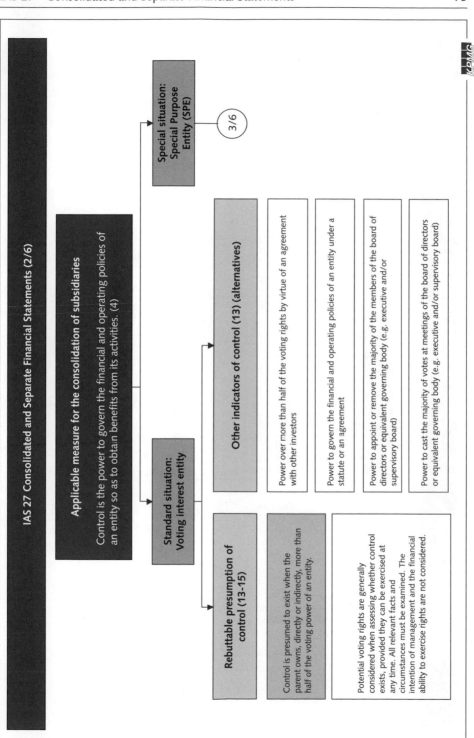

IAS 27 Consolidated and Separate Financial Statements (2/6)

Applicable measure for the consolidation of subsidiaries

Control is the power to govern the financial and operating policies of an entity so as to obtain benefits from its activities. (4)

Special situation: Special Purpose Entity (SPE)

3/6

Standard situation: Voting interest entity

Other indicators of control (13) (alternatives)

Power over more than half of the voting rights by virtue of an agreement with other investors

Power to govern the financial and operating policies of an entity under a statute or an agreement

Power to appoint or remove the majority of the members of the board of directors or equivalent governing body (e.g. executive and/or supervisory board)

Power to cast the majority of votes at meetings of the board of directors or equivalent governing body (e.g. executive and/or supervisory board)

Rebuttable presumption of control (13–15)

Control is presumed to exist when the parent owns, directly or indirectly, more than half of the voting power of an entity.

Potential voting rights are generally considered when assessing whether control exists, provided they can be exercised at any time. All relevant facts and circumstances must be examined. The intention of management and the financial ability to exercise rights are not considered.

IAS 27 Consolidated and Separate Financial Statements (3/6)

**Special situation:
Special Purpose Entity (SPE)**

Criteria for an SPE:

Created to accomplish a narrow and well-defined objective (SIC-12.1)

Strict and sometimes permanent limits on the decision-making powers of the governing body (SIC-12.1)

Extreme situation: autopilot (SIC-12.1)

The sponsor frequently transfers assets to the SPE, obtains the right to use assets held by the SPE, or performs services for the SPE (SIC-12.2)

Possible indicators of control: (SIC-12.10)

In substance, the activities of the SPE are being conducted on behalf of the entity according to its specific business needs so that the entity obtains benefits from the SPEs operation.

In substance, the entity has the decision-making powers to obtain the majority of the benefits of the activities of the SPE or, by setting up an autopilot mechanism, the entity has delegated these decision-making powers.

In substance, the entity has rights to obtain the majority of the benefits of the SPE and therefore may be exposed to risks incident to the activities of the SPE.

In substance, the entity retains the majority of the residual or ownership risks related to the SPE or its assets in order to obtain benefits from its activities.

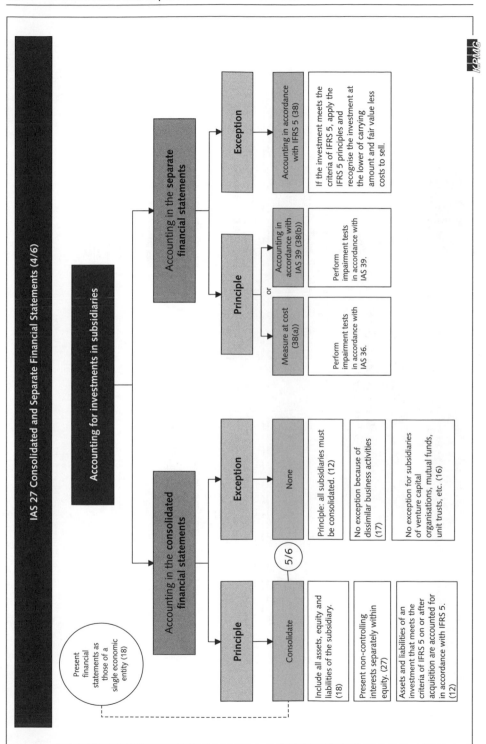

IAS 27 Consolidated and Separate Financial Statements (4/6)

Present financial statements as those of a single economic entity (18)

Accounting for investments in subsidiaries

Accounting in the consolidated financial statements

Principle

Consolidate

5/6

Include all assets, equity and liabilities of the subsidiary. (18)

Present non-controlling interests separately within equity. (27)

Assets and liabilities of an investment that meets the criteria of IFRS 5 on or after acquisition are accounted for in accordance with IFRS 5. (12)

Exception

None

Principle: all subsidiaries must be consolidated. (12)

No exception because of dissimilar business activities (17)

No exception for subsidiaries of venture capital organisations, mutual funds, unit trusts, etc. (16)

Accounting in the separate financial statements

Principle

Measure at cost (38(a))

Perform impairment tests in accordance with IAS 36.

or

Accounting in accordance with IAS 39 (38(b))

Perform impairment tests in accordance with IAS 39.

Exception

Accounting in accordance with IFRS 5 (38)

If the investment meets the criteria of IFRS 5, apply the IFRS 5 principles and recognise the investment at the lower of carrying amount and fair value less costs to sell.

KPMG

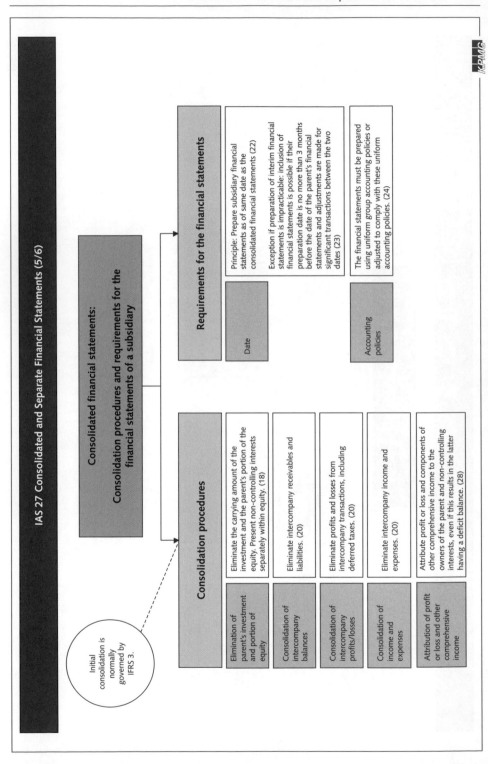

IAS 27 Consolidated and Separate Financial Statements (5/6)

Consolidated financial statements:

Consolidation procedures and requirements for the financial statements of a subsidiary

Initial consolidation is normally governed by IFRS 3.

Consolidation procedures

Elimination of parent's investment and portion of equity	Eliminate the carrying amount of the investment and the parent's portion of the equity. Present non-controlling interests separately within equity. (18)
Consolidation of intercompany balances	Eliminate intercompany receivables and liabilities. (20)
Consolidation of intercompany profits/losses	Eliminate profits and losses from intercompany transactions, including deferred taxes. (20)
Consolidation of income and expenses	Eliminate intercompany income and expenses. (20)
Attribution of profit or loss and other comprehensive income	Attribute profit or loss and components of other comprehensive income to the owners of the parent and non-controlling interests, even if this results in the latter having a deficit balance. (28)

Requirements for the financial statements

Date	Principle: Prepare subsidiary financial statements as of same date as the consolidated financial statements (22) Exception if preparation of interim financial statements is impracticable: inclusion of financial statements is possible if their preparation date is no more than 3 months before the date of the parent's financial statements and adjustments are made for significant transactions between the two dates (23)
Accounting policies	The financial statements must be prepared using uniform group accounting policies or adjusted to comply with these uniform accounting policies. (24)

KPMG

IAS 27 Consolidated and Separate Financial Statements (6/6)

Consolidated financial statements:

Consolidation after control is obtained, loss of control and other changes in the parent's ownership interest

Initial consolidation is normally governed by IFRS 3.

If appropriate, account for several legally separate transactions as a single transaction. (32, 33)

Consolidation after control is obtained (26)

Include income and expenses of the subsidiary in the consolidated financial statements from the acquisition date as defined in IFRS 3.

Base income and expenses on the values recognised in the consolidated financial statements at the acquisition date (generally carrying amounts from measurement in accordance with IFRS 3).

Other changes in parent's ownership interest (30, 31)

Account for changes in the ownership interest in a subsidiary that do not result in loss of control as equity transactions.

Adjust the carrying amounts of non-controlling interests to reflect any reduction in their interests in the subsidiary. Recognise any difference between the adjusted amount and the fair value of the consideration paid directly in equity and attribute it to the owners of the parent.

Adjust the carrying amounts of non-controlling interests to reflect any increase in their interests in the subsidiary. Recognise any difference between the adjusted amount and the fair value of the consideration received directly in equity and attribute it to the owners of the parent.

Loss of control (34–37)

Derecognise the carrying amounts in the consolidated financial statements at the date when control is lost:
- assets and liabilities of the subsidiary
- goodwill
- non-controlling interests

Recognise at fair value:
- the consideration received
- shares of the former subsidiary distributed to the owners and received by the entity
- any investment retained (recognise initially at fair value, and account for subsequently in accordance with other IFRSs)

Recognise any resulting difference as a gain or loss in profit or loss attributable to the owners of the parent.

Account for amounts previously recognised in other comprehensive income in accordance with other IFRSs as if for a disposal, i.e. either reclassify to profit or loss or transfer directly to retained earnings.

IAS 28 Investments in Associates
(amended 2008)

Scope: Accounting for investments in associates

Scope exclusions: Investments in associates held by venture capital organisations or similar entities that are measured at fair value in accordance with IAS 39

Core principles: An associate is an entity over which the investor has significant influence. Significant influence is the power to participate in the financial and operating policy decisions of the investee, but is not control or joint control over those policies.

Investments in associates are accounted for using the equity method in the consolidated financial statements. They are initially recognised at cost, and the carrying amount is adjusted in subsequent periods to reflect changes in the investor's share of the associate's net assets. Any goodwill included in the carrying amount of the investment is not amortised, and the entire carrying amount is tested for impairment in accordance with IAS 39 and IAS 36.

If the investment meets the criteria of IFRS 5 for classification as an asset held for sale, it is accounted for in accordance with IFRS 5.

In 'separate financial statements' (single-entity financial statements prepared in accordance with IFRSs), investments in associates must be accounted for consistently for each category of investment either at cost or in accordance with IAS 39.

Effective date: Annual periods beginning on or after 1 January 2005. Earlier application is encouraged. Amendments resulting from IAS 1 (amended 2007) and IAS 27 (amended 2008) must be applied at the same time as the amended IAS 1 and IAS 27 respectively.

Applies to: All entities

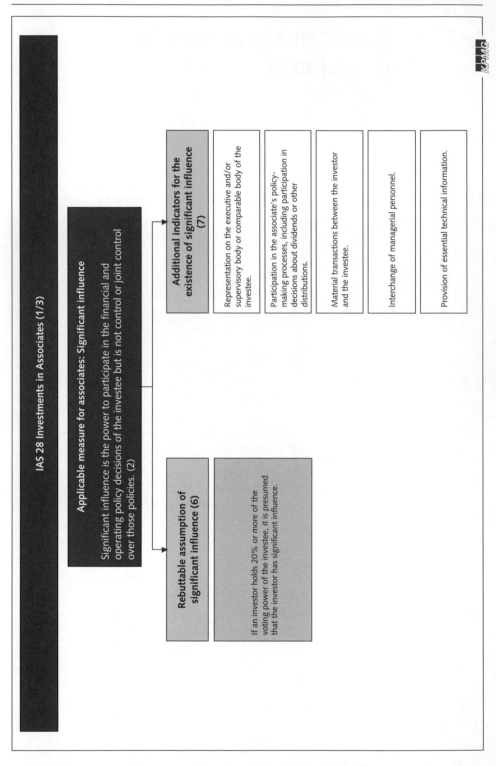

IAS 28 Investments in Associates (1/3)

Applicable measure for associates: Significant influence

Significant influence is the power to participate in the financial and operating policy decisions of the investee but is not control or joint control over those policies. (2)

Rebuttable assumption of significant influence (6)

If an investor holds 20% or more of the voting power of the investee, it is presumed that the investor has significant influence.

Additional indicators for the existence of significant influence (7)

Representation on the executive and/or supervisory body or comparable body of the investee.

Participation in the associate's policy-making processes, including participation in decisions about dividends or other distributions.

Material transactions between the investor and the investee.

Interchange of managerial personnel.

Provision of essential technical information.

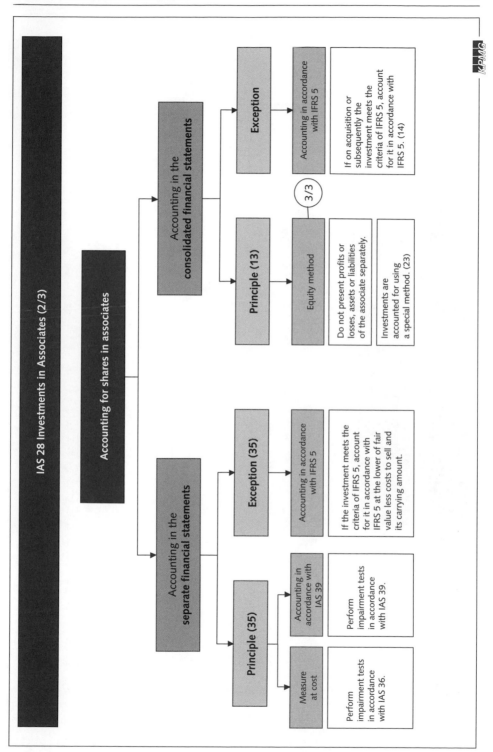

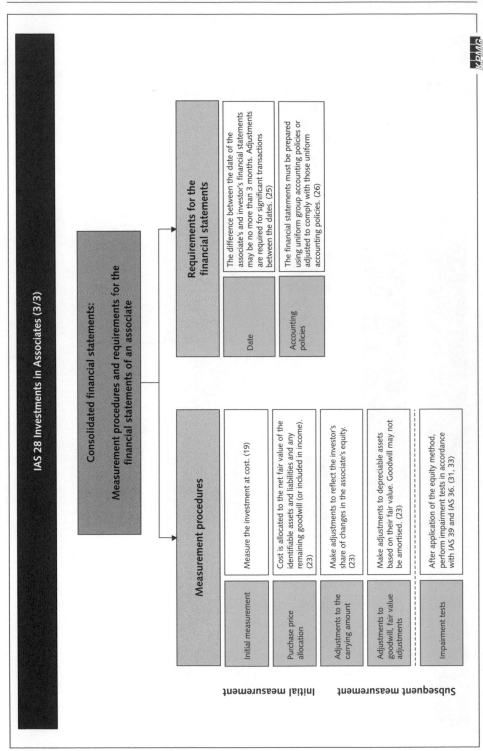

IAS 28 Investments in Associates (3/3)

Consolidated financial statements:

Measurement procedures and requirements for the financial statements of an associate

Requirements for the financial statements

| Date | The difference between the date of the associate's and investor's financial statements may be no more than 3 months. Adjustments are required for significant transactions between the dates. (25) |
| Accounting policies | The financial statements must be prepared using uniform group accounting policies or adjusted to comply with those uniform accounting policies. (26) |

Measurement procedures

Initial measurement	Measure the investment at cost. (19)
Purchase price allocation	Cost is allocated to the net fair value of the identifiable assets and liabilities and any remaining goodwill (or included in income). (23)
Adjustments to the carrying amount	Make adjustments to reflect the investor's share of changes in the associate's equity. (23)
Adjustments to goodwill, fair value adjustments	Make adjustments to depreciable assets based on their fair value. Goodwill may not be amortised. (23)
Impairment tests	After application of the equity method, perform impairment tests in accordance with IAS 39 and IAS 36. (31, 33)

Initial measurement

Subsequent measurement

IAS 29 Financial Reporting in Hyperinflationary Economies
(amended 2007)

Scope: Restatement of the primary financial statements of an entity that prepares its financial statements in the currency of a hyperinflationary economy.

Scope exclusions: –

Core principles: Hyperinflation may be indicated by a number of features, for example where the cumulative inflation rate over three years is approaching, or exceeds, 100%.

The financial statements of an entity whose functional currency is the currency of a hyperinflationary economy are restated to reflect the conditions prevailing at the end of the reporting period. Statement of financial position amounts that are not already expressed in terms of a monetary measuring unit, and that are not governed by agreements linked to changes in prices or carried at current cost, are restated by applying a general price index.

The net amount of these adjustments are recognised in profit or loss and disclosed separately in the notes.

Effective date: Annual periods beginning on or after 1 January 1990.

Applies to: All entities

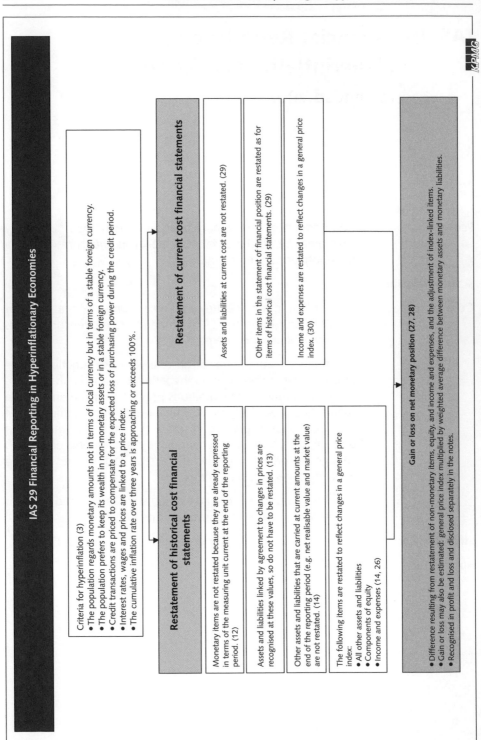

IAS 29 Financial Reporting in Hyperinflationary Economies

Criteria for hyperinflation (3)
- The population regards monetary amounts not in terms of local currency but in terms of a stable foreign currency.
- The population prefers to keep its wealth in non-monetary assets or in a stable foreign currency.
- Credit transactions are priced to compensate for the expected loss of purchasing power during the credit period.
- Interest rates, wages and prices are linked to a price index.
- The cumulative inflation rate over three years is approaching or exceeds 100%.

Restatement of historical cost financial statements

Monetary items are not restated because they are already expressed in terms of the measuring unit current at the end of the reporting period. (12)

Assets and liabilities linked by agreement to changes in prices are recognised at these values, so do not have to be restated. (13)

Other assets and liabilities that are carried at current amounts at the end of the reporting period (e.g. net realisable value and market value) are not restated. (14)

The following items are restated to reflect changes in a general price index:
- All other assets and liabilities
- Components of equity
- Income and expenses (14, 26)

Restatement of current cost financial statements

Assets and liabilities at current cost are not restated. (29)

Other items in the statement of financial position are restated as for items of historical cost financial statements. (29)

Income and expenses are restated to reflect changes in a general price index. (30)

Gain or loss on net monetary position (27, 28)

- Difference resulting from restatement of non-monetary items, equity, and income and expenses, and the adjustment of index-linked items.
- Gain or loss may also be estimated: general price index multiplied by weighted average difference between monetary assets and monetary liabilities.
- Recognised in profit and loss and disclosed separately in the notes.

IAS 31 Interests in Joint Ventures
(amended 2008)

Scope:	Accounting for interests in joint ventures
Scope exclusions:	Interests in joint ventures held by venture capital organisations or similar entities
Core principles:	Joint ventures (in the sense of 'jointly controlled entities') are legally independent entities that are controlled jointly by the reporting entity together with one or more partners. Joint control requires a contractual arrangement and therefore differs from significant influence. Other forms of joint ventures are jointly controlled operations and jointly controlled assets.
	Interests in joint ventures (in the sense of 'jointly controlled entities') are recognised consistently in the consolidated financial statements either by proportionate consolidation or by using the equity method. In proportionate consolidation, the venturer's share of the assets and liabilities of the joint venture ('jointly controlled entity'), and its income and expenses, are included in the venturer's consolidated financial statements on a line by line basis. The carrying amount of the interest in the joint venture is eliminated against the venturer's share of the joint venture's equity. Intragroup transactions and balances are eliminated proportionately using the same procedures as set out in IAS 27. Application of the equity method follows the procedures set out in IAS 28.
	In 'separate financial statements' (single-entity financial statements prepared in accordance with IFRSs), interests in joint ventures must be accounted for either at cost or in accordance with IAS 39. The method used should be applied consistently to each category of investment.
Effective date:	Annual periods beginning on or after 1 January 2005. Earlier application is encouraged. Amendments resulting from IAS 27 (amended 2008) must be applied at the same time as the amended IAS 27.
Applies to:	All entities

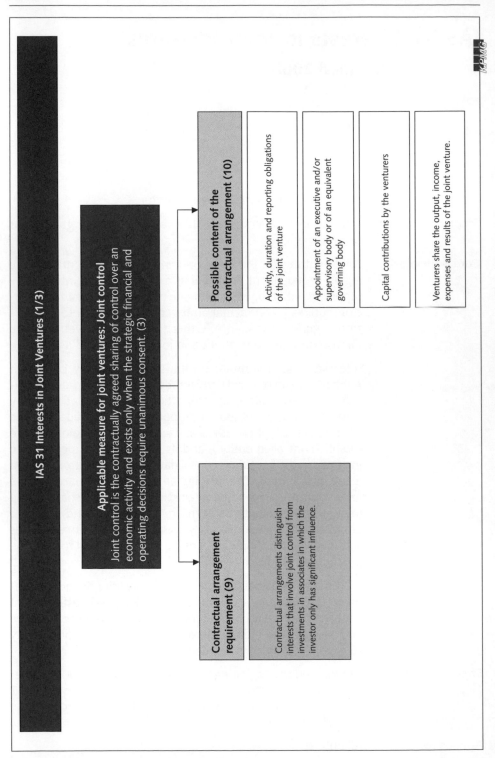

IAS 31 Interests in Joint Ventures (1/3)

Applicable measure for joint ventures: Joint control

Joint control is the contractually agreed sharing of control over an economic activity and exists only when the strategic financial and operating decisions require unanimous consent. (3)

Possible content of the contractual arrangement (10)

Activity, duration and reporting obligations of the joint venture

Appointment of an executive and/or supervisory body or of an equivalent governing body

Capital contributions by the venturers

Venturers share the output, income, expenses and results of the joint venture.

Contractual arrangement requirement (9)

Contractual arrangements distinguish interests that involve joint control from investments in associates in which the investor only has significant influence.

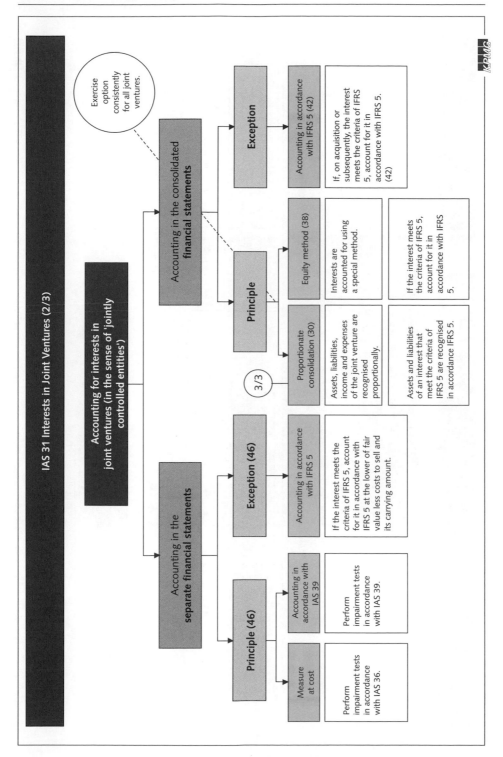

IAS 31 Interests in Joint Ventures (2/3)

Accounting for interests in joint ventures (in the sense of 'jointly controlled entities')

Accounting in the consolidated financial statements

Exercise option consistently for all joint ventures.

Exception

Accounting in accordance with IFRS 5 (42)

If, on acquisition or subsequently, the interest meets the criteria of IFRS 5, account for it in accordance with IFRS 5. (42)

Principle

Equity method (38)

Interests are accounted for using a special method.

If the interest meets the criteria of IFRS 5, account for it in accordance with IFRS 5.

Proportionate consolidation (30)

3/3

Assets, liabilities, income and expenses of the joint venture are recognised proportionally.

Assets and liabilities of an interest that meet the criteria of IFRS 5 are recognised in accordance IFRS 5.

Accounting in the separate financial statements

Exception (46)

Accounting in accordance with IFRS 5

If the interest meets the criteria of IFRS 5, account for it in accordance with IFRS 5 at the lower of fair value less costs to sell and its carrying amount.

Principle (46)

Accounting in accordance with IAS 39

Perform impairment tests in accordance with IAS 39.

Measure at cost

Perform impairment tests in accordance with IAS 36.

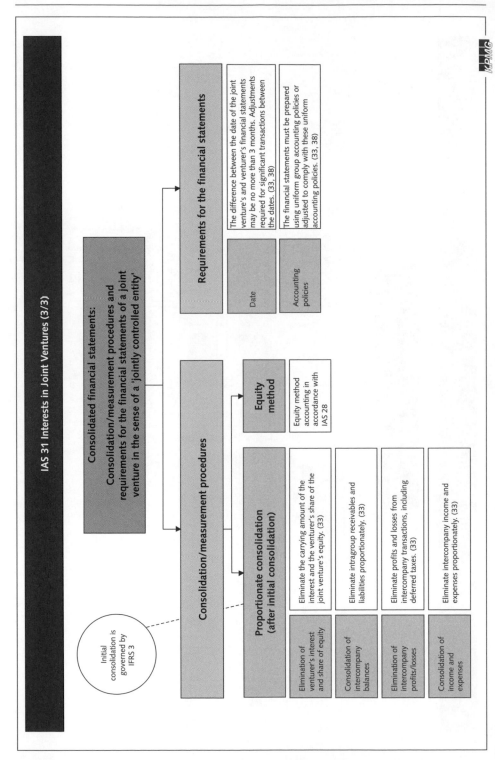

IAS 31 Interests in Joint Ventures (3/3)

Consolidated financial statements:

Consolidation/measurement procedures and requirements for the financial statements of a joint venture in the sense of a 'jointly controlled entity'

Requirements for the financial statements

Date — The difference between the date of the joint venture's and venturer's financial statements may be no more than 3 months. Adjustments required for significant transactions between the dates. (33, 38)

Accounting policies — The financial statements must be prepared using uniform group accounting policies or adjusted to comply with these uniform accounting policies. (33, 38)

Consolidation/measurement procedures

Equity method

Equity method accounting in accordance with IAS 28

Proportionate consolidation (after initial consolidation)

Elimination of venturer's interest and share of equity — Eliminate the carrying amount of the interest and the venturer's share of the joint venture's equity. (33)

Consolidation of intercompany balances — Eliminate intragroup receivables and liabilities proportionately. (33)

Elimination of intercompany profits/losses — Eliminate profits and losses from intercompany transactions, including deferred taxes. (33)

Consolidation of income and expenses — Eliminate intercompany income and expenses proportionately. (33)

Initial consolidation is governed by IFRS 3

IAS 32 Financial Instruments: Presentation

(amended 2008)

Scope: Presentation of information about financial instruments

Scope exclusions: Interests in subsidiaries, associates and joint ventures that are not accounted for using IAS 39; employers' obligations under post-employment benefit plans and, as a rule, under stock option plans; obligations arising under insurance contracts; and contracts for contingent consideration in a business combination.

Core principles: IAS 32 governs the following presentation issues: the presentation of financial instruments by the issuer as equity or liability depending on the substance of the contractual arrangement; the recognition of interest and dividends as expense or income, or directly in equity; the requirement to offset financial assets and liabilities in the statement of financial position if certain criteria are met.

Effective date: Annual periods beginning on or after 1 January 2005. Earlier application is permitted in conjunction with the application of IAS 39 (amended 2003). Amendments resulting from IAS 1 (amended 2007) and IFRS 3 (amended 2008) must be applied at the same time as the amended IAS 1 and IFRS 3 respectively.

Applies to: All entities

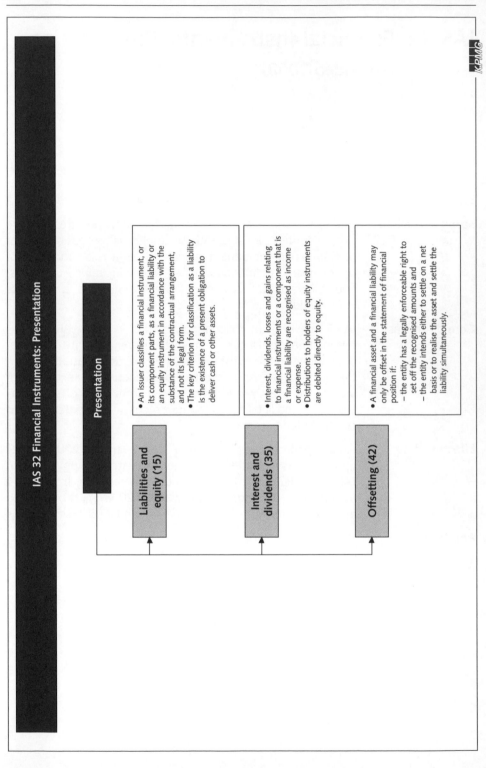

IAS 32 Financial Instruments: Presentation

Presentation

Liabilities and equity (15)

- An issuer classifies a financial instrument, or its component parts, as a financial liability or an equity instrument in accordance with the substance of the contractual arrangement, and not its legal form.
- The key criterion for classification as a liability is the existence of a present obligation to deliver cash or other assets.

Interest and dividends (35)

- Interest, dividends, losses and gains relating to financial instruments or a component that is a financial liability are recognised as income or expense.
- Distributions to holders of equity instruments are debited directly to equity.

Offsetting (42)

- A financial asset and a financial liability may only be offset in the statement of financial position if:
  - the entity has a legally enforceable right to set off the recognised amounts and
  - the entity intends either to settle on a net basis or to realise the asset and settle the liability simultaneously.

IAS 33 Earnings per Share (amended 2007)

Scope:	Determination and presentation of earnings per share
Scope exclusions:	–
Core principles:	Basic earnings per share are calculated by dividing profit or loss for the period attributable to the shareholders of the parent, less the after-tax amount of any preference dividends payable for the period, by the weighted average number of ordinary shares outstanding during the period. These disclosures must be provided separately for each class of ordinary shares.
	Diluted earnings per share differ from basic earnings per share in that the numerator (profit or loss) and denominator (number of shares) are adjusted by the hypothetical effect of converting all dilutive potential ordinary shares. A potential ordinary share is a financial instrument or other contract that may entitle its holder to ordinary shares. Potential ordinary shares are dilutive if their conversion would reduce earnings per share (from continuing operations).
	Both basic and diluted earnings per share must be presented in the statement of comprehensive income or in the income statement (if presented separately) and explained in the notes. In the case of discontinued operations, the disclosure on the face of the statement of comprehensive income/income statement refers to earnings from continuing operations; at a minimum, earnings per share for discontinued operations must be disclosed in the notes.
Effective date:	Annual periods beginning on or after 1 January 2005. Earlier application is encouraged. Amendments resulting from IAS 1 (amended 2007) must be applied at the same time as the amended IAS 1.
Applies to:	Publicly traded entities only

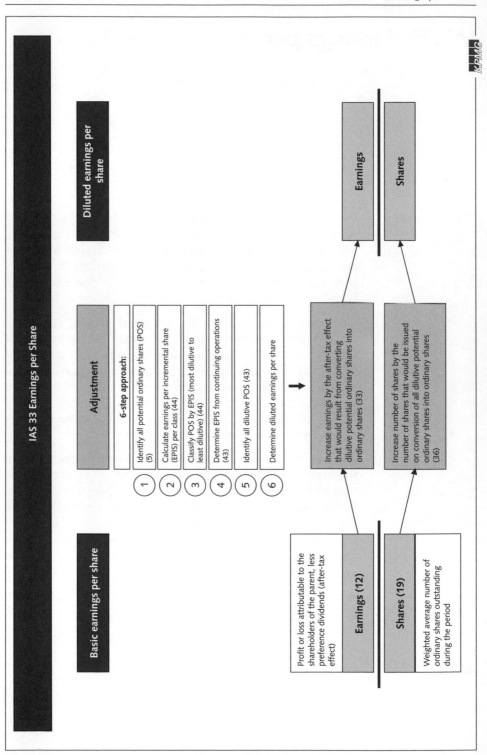

IAS 34 Interim Financial Reporting
(amended 2008)

Scope: Minimum content and presentation of interim financial reports; recognition and measurement policies to be applied

Scope exclusions: IAS 34 does not specify which entities are required to publish interim financial statement

Core principles: An interim financial report contains the same primary statements as year-end financial statements (statement of financial position, statement of comprehensive income, statement of changes in equity and statement of cash flows). The statements can be presented in complete or condensed forms. Selected explanatory notes are also required.

Entities should apply the same accounting policies in interim financial statements as are applied in the most recent annual financial statements, except for accounting policy changes made after the prior period end that are to be reflected in the next annual financial statements. Measurements in interim financial reports may require a greater use of estimates.

Effective date: Annual periods beginning on or after 1 January 1999. Amendments resulting from IAS 1 (amended 2007) and IFRS 3 (amended 2008) must be applied at the same time as the amended IAS 1 and IFRS 3 respectively.

Applies to: All entities required by law or contractual stipulations (e.g. stock exchange rules and regulations, articles of association, local commercial or company law) to prepare an interim financial report in accordance with IFRSs.

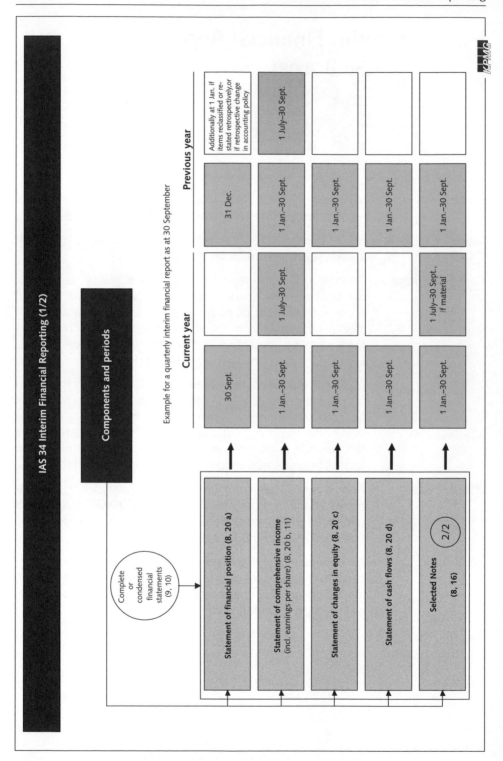

IAS 34 Interim Financial Reporting (1/2)

Components and periods

Example for a quarterly interim financial report as at 30 September

Complete or condensed financial statements (9, 10)	Current year		Previous year	
	30 Sept.		31 Dec.	Additionally at 1 Jan. if items reclassified or restated retrospectively, or if retrospective change in accounting policy
Statement of financial position (8, 20 a)	1 Jan.–30 Sept.	1 July–30 Sept.	1 Jan.–30 Sept.	1 July–30 Sept.
Statement of comprehensive income (incl. earnings per share) (8, 20 b, 11)	1 Jan.–30 Sept.		1 Jan.–30 Sept.	
Statement of changes in equity (8, 20 c)	1 Jan.–30 Sept.		1 Jan.–30 Sept.	
Statement of cash flows (8, 20 d)	1 Jan.–30 Sept.	1 July–30 Sept., if material	1 Jan.–30 Sept.	
Selected Notes (8, 16)				

2/2

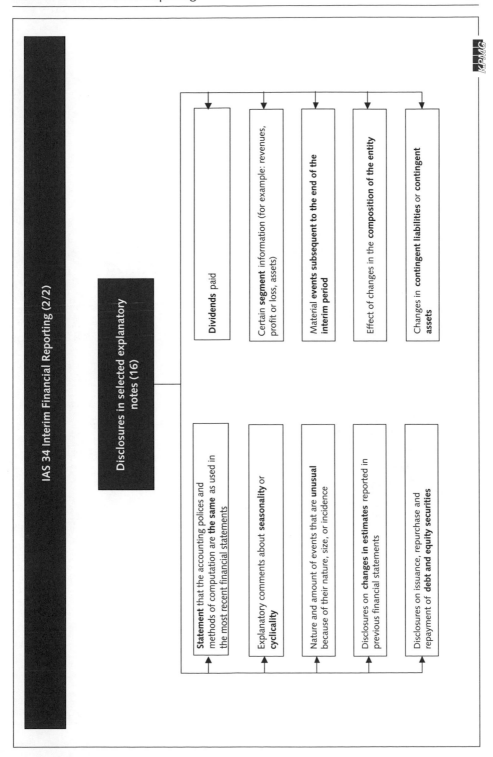

IAS 34 Interim Financial Reporting (2/2)

Disclosures in selected explanatory notes (16)

Statement that the accounting polices and methods of computation are **the same** as used in the most recent financial statements

Explanatory comments about **seasonality** or **cyclicality**

Nature and amount of events that are **unusual** because of their nature, size, or incidence

Disclosures on **changes in estimates** reported in previous financial statements

Disclosures on issuance, repurchase and repayment of **debt and equity securities**

Dividends paid

Certain **segment** information (for example: revenues, profit or loss, assets)

Material **events subsequent to the end of the interim period**

Effect of changes in the **composition of the entity**

Changes in **contingent liabilities** or **contingent assets**

KPMG

IAS 36 Impairment of Assets (amended 2008)

Scope: Accounting for the impairment of assets

Scope exclusions: Inventories, assets arising from construction contracts, deferred tax assets, assets associated with future employee benefits, financial assets that are within the scope of IAS 39, investment property measured at fair value, biological assets, and certain assets arising from insurance contracts.

Core principles: The assets covered by IAS 36 (in particular intangible assets and property, plant and equipment) must be assessed at the end of each reporting period to establish whether there are indications that they may be impaired. An impairment test must be performed if there are indications of impairment. An impairment test must be performed for goodwill and certain intangible assets annually.

An asset is impaired if its carrying amount is higher than its recoverable amount. An asset's recoverable amount is the higher of its fair value less costs to sell and its value in use. Value in use is the present (discounted) value of the future cash flows expected to be derived from an asset (future cash inflows less the cash outflows needed to generate the inflows). If an asset is impaired, an impairment loss is generally recognised in profit and loss. The carrying amount is then assessed in future periods to establish whether the asset is still impaired. If it is no longer impaired, the impairment loss is reversed (except in the case of goodwill impairment). If an asset does not itself generate cash flows, the cash-generating unit (CGU) to which it belongs is tested for impairment.

Effective date: Applies to goodwill and intangible assets acquired in business combinations after 31 March 2004, and to all other assets for annual periods beginning on or after 31 March 2004. Amendments resulting from IAS 1 (amended 2007) and IFRS 3 (amended 2008) must be applied at the same time as the amended IAS 1 and IFRS 3 respectively.

Applies to: All entities

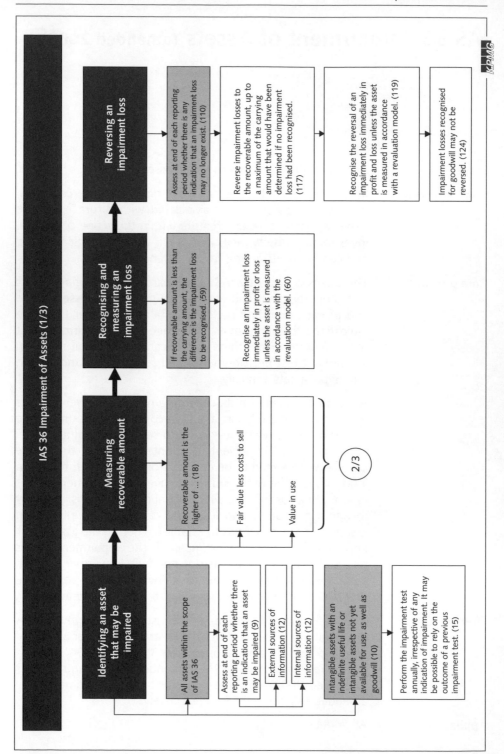

IAS 36 Impairment of Assets (1/3)

Identifying an asset that may be impaired

All assets within the scope of IAS 36

Assess at end of each reporting period whether there is an indication that an asset may be impaired (9)

External sources of information (12)

Internal sources of information (12)

Intangible assets with an indefinite useful life or intangible assets not yet available for use, as well as goodwill (10)

Perform the impairment test annually, irrespective of any indication of impairment. It may be possible to rely on the outcome of a previous impairment test. (15)

Measuring recoverable amount

Recoverable amount is the higher of ... (18)

Fair value less costs to sell

Value in use

2/3

Recognising and measuring an impairment loss

If recoverable amount is less than the carrying amount, the difference is the impairment loss to be recognised. (59)

Recognise an impairment loss immediately in profit or loss unless the asset is measured in accordance with the revaluation model. (60)

Reversing an impairment loss

Assess at end of each reporting period whether there is any indication that an impairment loss may no longer exist. (110)

Reverse impairment losses to the recoverable amount, up to a maximum of the carrying amount that would have been determined if no impairment loss had been recognised. (117)

Recognise the reversal of an impairment loss immediately in profit and loss unless the asset is measured in accordance with a revaluation model. (119)

Impairment losses recognised for goodwill may not be reversed. (124)

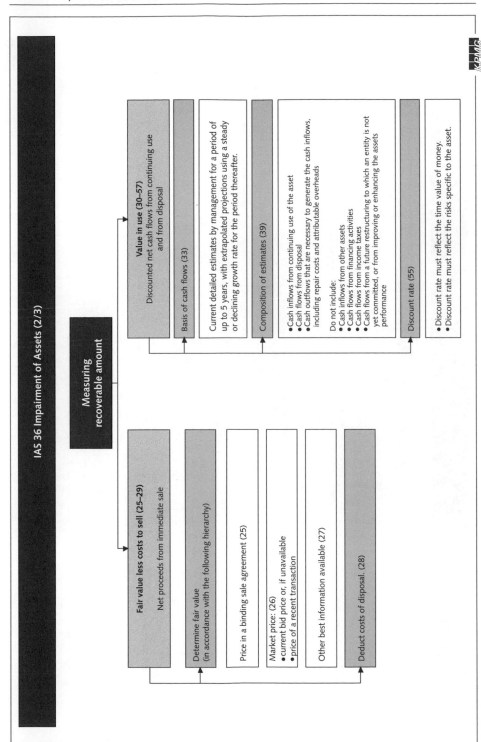

IAS 36 Impairment of Assets (2/3)

Measuring recoverable amount

Value in use (30–57)

Discounted net cash flows from continuing use and from disposal

Basis of cash flows (33)

Current detailed estimates by management for a period of up to 5 years, with extrapolated projections using a steady or declining growth rate for the period thereafter.

Composition of estimates (39)

- Cash inflows from continuing use of the asset
- Cash flows from disposal
- Cash outflows that are necessary to generate the cash inflows, including repair costs and attributable overheads

Do not include:
- Cash inflows from other assets
- Cash flows from financing activities
- Cash flows from income taxes
- Cash flows from a future restructuring to which an entity is not yet committed, or from improving or enhancing the assets performance

Discount rate (55)

- Discount rate must reflect the time value of money.
- Discount rate must reflect the risks specific to the asset.

Fair value less costs to sell (25–29)

Net proceeds from immediate sale

Determine fair value
(in accordance with the following hierarchy)

Price in a binding sale agreement (25)

Market price: (26)
- current bid price or, if unavailable
- price of a recent transaction

Other best information available (27)

Deduct costs of disposal. (28)

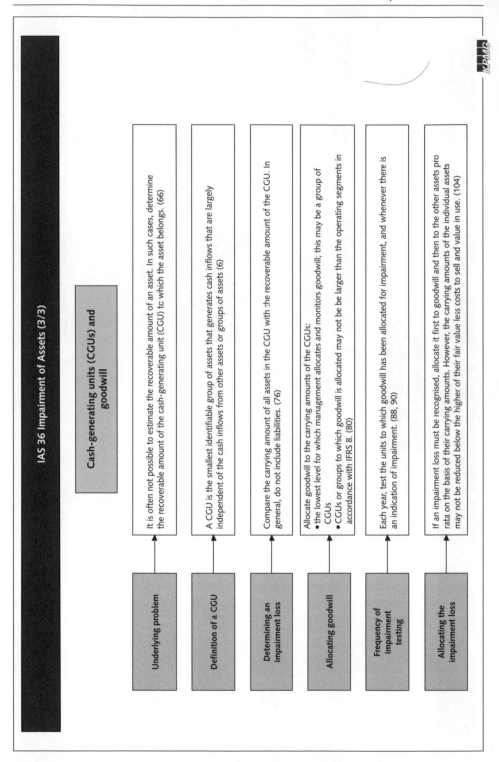

IAS 36 Impairment of Assets (3/3)

Cash-generating units (CGUs) and goodwill

Underlying problem
It is often not possible to estimate the recoverable amount of an asset. In such cases, determine the recoverable amount of the cash-generating unit (CGU) to which the asset belongs. (66)

Definition of a CGU
A CGU is the smallest identifiable group of assets that generates cash inflows that are largely independent of the cash inflows from other assets or groups of assets (6)

Determining an impairment loss
Compare the carrying amount of all assets in the CGU with the recoverable amount of the CGU. In general, do not include liabilities. (76)

Allocating goodwill
Allocate goodwill to the carrying amounts of the CGUs:
• the lowest level for which management allocates and monitors goodwill; this may be a group of CGUs
• CGUs or groups to which goodwill is allocated may not be larger than the operating segments in accordance with IFRS 8. (80)

Frequency of impairment testing
Each year, test the units to which goodwill has been allocated for impairment, and whenever there is an indication of impairment. (88, 90)

Allocating the impairment loss
If an impairment loss must be recognised, allocate it first to goodwill and then to the other assets pro rata on the basis of their carrying amounts. However, the carrying amounts of the individual assets may not be reduced below the higher of their fair value less costs to sell and value in use. (104)

IAS 37 Provisions, Contingent Liabilities and Contingent Assets (amended 2008)

Scope:	Accounting for provisions, contingent liabilities and contingent assets
Scope exclusions:	Financial instruments that are within the scope of IAS 39; executory contracts, except where the contracts are onerous; obligations at insurers from contracts with policyholders; obligations (e.g. income taxes, employee benefits) covered by another standard.
Core principles:	Provisions are present obligations (legal or constructive) arising as a result of past events, whose settlement will probably require an outflow of resources, and whose amount can be estimated reliably.
	They are measured by applying the 'best estimate': the amount recognised as a provision is the best estimate of the expenditure required to settle the present obligation at the end of the reporting period. The obligation is discounted at a current (pre-tax) market rate of interest for similar maturities if the effect of the time value of money is material. Future events that may affect the amount required to settle an obligation are reflected in the amount of the provision if there is sufficient objective evidence that they will occur. Claims for reimbursement may not be deducted from the carrying amount of the provision, but amounts reimbursed may be offset in the statement of comprehensive income. Specific accounting principles apply to future operating losses, expected losses from onerous contracts and restructuring provisions.
	Contingent liabilities and contingent assets are only disclosed in the notes.
Effective date:	Annual periods beginning on or after 1 July 1999.
Applies to:	All entities

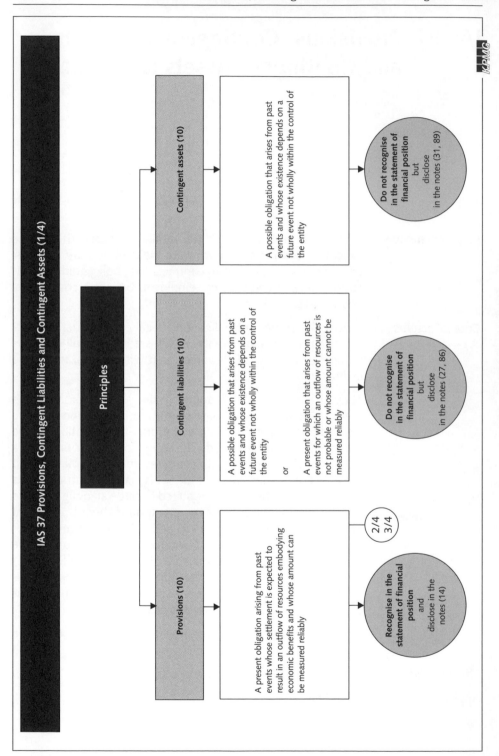

IAS 37 Provisions, Contingent Liabilities and Contingent Assets (1/4)

Principles

Provisions (10)

A present obligation arising from past events whose settlement is expected to result in an outflow of resources embodying economic benefits and whose amount can be measured reliably

Recognise in the statement of financial position and disclose in the notes (14)

Contingent liabilities (10)

A possible obligation that arises from past events and whose existence depends on a future event not wholly within the control of the entity

or

A present obligation that arises from past events for which an outflow of resources is not probable or whose amount cannot be measured reliably

Do not recognise in the statement of financial position but disclose in the notes (27, 86)

Contingent assets (10)

A possible obligation that arises from past events and whose existence depends on a future event not wholly within the control of the entity

Do not recognise in the statement of financial position but disclose in the notes (31, 89)

2/4
3/4

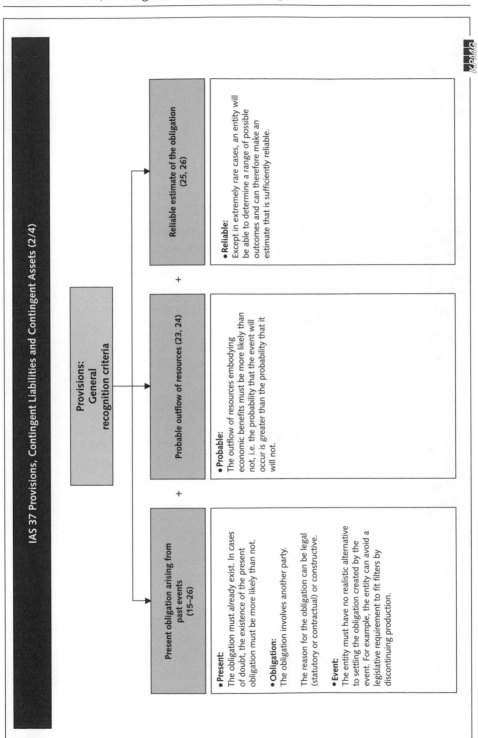

IAS 37 Provisions, Contingent Liabilities and Contingent Assets (2/4)

**Provisions:
General
recognition criteria**

**Present obligation arising from past events
(15–26)**

+

Probable outflow of resources (23, 24)

+

**Reliable estimate of the obligation
(25, 26)**

● **Present:**
The obligation must already exist. In cases of doubt, the existence of the present obligation must be more likely than not.

● **Obligation:**
The obligation involves another party.

The reason for the obligation can be legal (statutory or contractual) or constructive.

● **Event:**
The entity must have no realistic alternative to settling the obligation created by the event. For example, the entity can avoid a legislative requirement to fit filters by discontinuing production.

● **Probable:**
The outflow of resources embodying economic benefits must be more likely than not, i.e. the probability that the event will occur is greater than the probability that it will not.

● **Reliable:**
Except in extremely rare cases, an entity will be able to determine a range of possible outcomes and can therefore make an estimate that is sufficiently reliable.

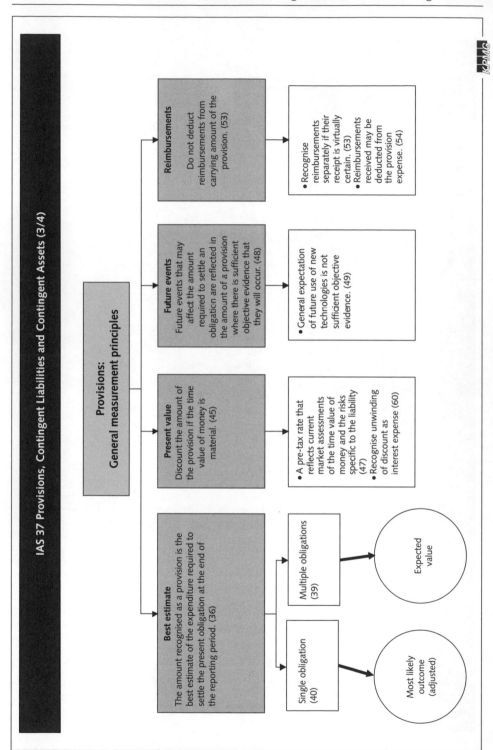

IAS 37 Provisions, Contingent Liabilities and Contingent Assets (3/4)

Provisions:
General measurement principles

Best estimate
The amount recognised as a provision is the best estimate of the expenditure required to settle the present obligation at the end of the reporting period. (36)

Single obligation (40)

Multiple obligations (39)

Most likely outcome (adjusted)

Expected value

Present value
Discount the amount of the provision if the time value of money is material. (45)

- A pre-tax rate that reflects current market assessments of the time value of money and the risks specific to the liability (47)
- Recognise unwinding of discount as interest expense (60)

Future events
Future events that may affect the amount required to settle an obligation are reflected in the amount of a provision where there is sufficient objective evidence that they will occur. (48)

- General expectation of future use of new technologies is not sufficient objective evidence. (49)

Reimbursements
Do not deduct reimbursements from carrying amount of the provision. (53)

- Recognise reimbursements separately if their receipt is virtually certain. (53)
- Reimbursements received may be deducted from the provision expense. (54)

KPMG

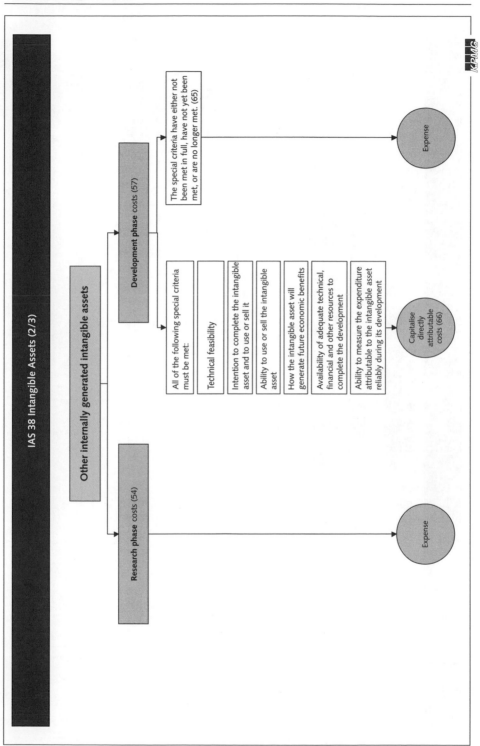

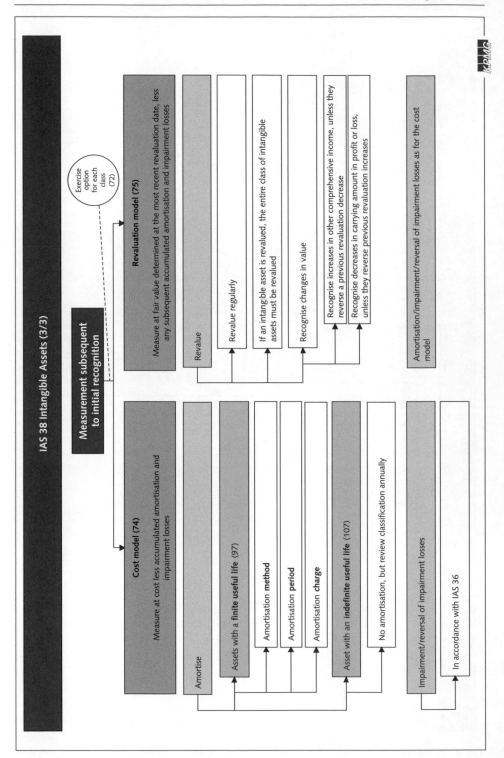

IAS 38 Intangible Assets (3/3)

Measurement subsequent to initial recognition

Exercise option for each class (72)

Cost model (74)
Measure at cost less accumulated amortisation and impairment losses

Amortise

Assets with a finite useful life (97)

Amortisation **method**

Amortisation **period**

Amortisation **charge**

Asset with an **indefinite useful life** (107)

No amortisation, but review classification annually

Impairment/reversal of impairment losses

In accordance with IAS 36

Revaluation model (75)
Measure at fair value determined at the most recent revaluation date, less any subsequent accumulated amortisation and impairment losses

Revalue

Revalue regularly

If an intangible asset is revalued, the entire class of intangible assets must be revalued

Recognise changes in value

Recognise increases in other comprehensive income, unless they reverse a previous revaluation decrease

Recognise decreases in carrying amount in profit or loss, unless they reverse previous revaluation increases

Amortisation/impairment/reversal of impairment losses as for the cost model

KPMG

IAS 39 Financial Instruments: Recognition and Measurement (amended 2008)

Scope:	Recognition and measurement of financial instruments
Scope exclusions:	Numerous
Core principles:	Financial assets are classified into four categories: financial assets at fair value through profit or loss, held-to-maturity investments, loans and receivables, and available-for-sale financial assets. Assets in the first and last categories are generally measured at fair value, although there are differences in the way changes in fair value are recognised. Assets in the other categories are measured at amortised cost.
	In addition to the classification of financial assets based on their nature (primary classification), certain assets may also be assigned to different categories on initial recognition if certain criteria are met (designation options). This applies in particular to the 'fair value option'.
	Financial liabilities are classified into financial liabilities measured at amortised cost and financial liabilities at fair value through profit or loss.
	Hedge accounting may be applied to hedges in which a hedging instrument is formally allocated to a hedged item (underlying). Hedges are classified into three categories. The hedging instrument and the hedged item are analysed separately, and may also be accounted for separately. One of the consequences of hedge accounting is that, to the extent that the hedge is effective, gains and losses are offset in profit or loss.
Effective date:	Annual periods beginning on or after 1 January 2005, with numerous specific requirements. Amendments resulting from IAS 1 (amended 2007), IAS 27 (amended 2008) and IFRS 3 (amended 2008) must be applied at the same time as the amended IAS 1, IAS 27 and IFRS 3 respectively.
Applies to:	All entities

IAS 39 Financial Instruments: Recognition and Measurement (1/7)

Classification of financial assets

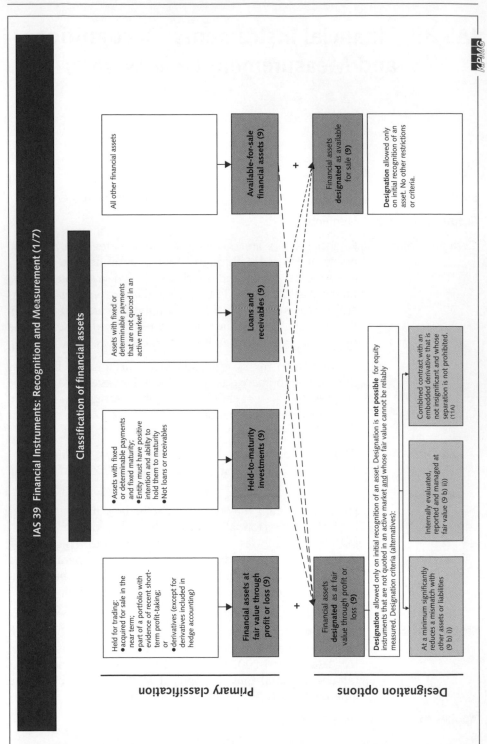

Primary classification

- Held for trading:
  - acquired for sale in the near term;
  - part of a portfolio with evidence of recent short-term profit-taking; or
  - derivatives (except for derivatives included in hedge accounting)

Financial assets at fair value through profit or loss (9)

- Assets with fixed or determinable payments and fixed maturity;
  - Entity must have positive intention and ability to hold them to maturity
  - Not loans or receivables

Held-to-maturity investments (9)

Assets with fixed or determinable payments that are not quoted in an active market.

Loans and receivables (9)

All other financial assets

Available-for-sale financial assets (9)

Designation options

+

Financial assets designated as at fair value through profit or loss (9)

Designation allowed only on initial recognition of an asset. Designation is **not possible** for equity instruments that are not quoted in an active market _and_ whose fair value cannot be reliably measured. Designation criteria (alternatives):

- At a minimum significantly reduces a mismatch with other assets or liabilities (9 b) i))
- Internally evaluated, reported and managed at fair value (9 b) ii))
- Combined contract with an embedded derivative that is not insignificant and whose separation is not prohibited. (11A)

+

Financial assets designated as available for sale (9)

Designation allowed only on initial recognition of an asset. No other restrictions or criteria.

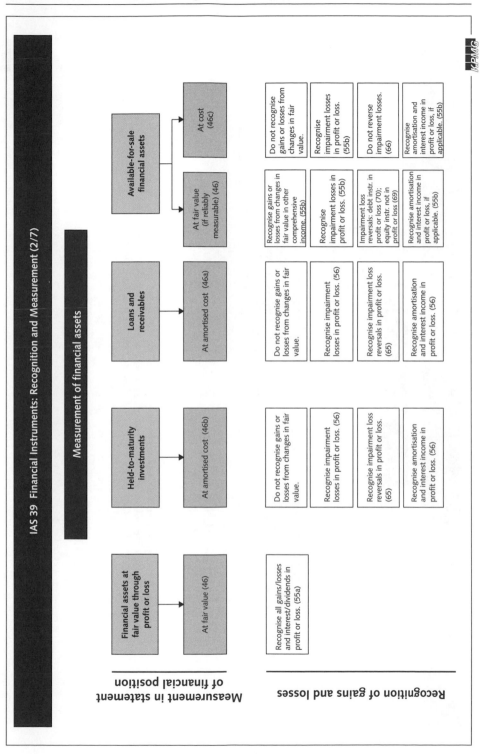

IAS 39 Financial Instruments: Recognition and Measurement (2/7)

Measurement of financial assets

Measurement in statement of financial position

Financial assets at fair value through profit or loss	Held-to-maturity investments	Loans and receivables	Available-for-sale financial assets
At fair value (46)	At amortised cost (46b)	At amortised cost (46a)	At fair value (if reliably measurable) (46) / At cost (46c)

Recognition of gains and losses

Financial assets at fair value through profit or loss:
- Recognise all gains/losses and interest/dividends in profit or loss. (55a)

Held-to-maturity investments:
- Do not recognise gains or losses from changes in fair value.
- Recognise impairment losses in profit or loss. (56)
- Recognise impairment loss reversals in profit or loss. (65)
- Recognise amortisation and interest income in profit or loss. (56)

Loans and receivables:
- Do not recognise gains or losses from changes in fair value.
- Recognise impairment losses in profit or loss. (56)
- Recognise impairment loss reversals in profit or loss. (65)
- Recognise amortisation and interest income in profit or loss. (56)

Available-for-sale financial assets (at fair value):
- Recognise gains or losses from changes in fair value in other comprehensive income. (55b)
- Recognise impairment losses in profit or loss. (55b)
- Impairment loss reversals: debt instr. in profit or loss (70); equity instr. not in profit or loss (69)
- Recognise amortisation and interest income in profit or loss, if applicable. (55b)

Available-for-sale financial assets (at cost):
- Do not recognise gains or losses from changes in fair value.
- Recognise impairment losses in profit or loss. (55b)
- Do not reverse impairment losses. (66)
- Recognise amortisation and interest income in profit or loss, if applicable. (55b)

KPMG

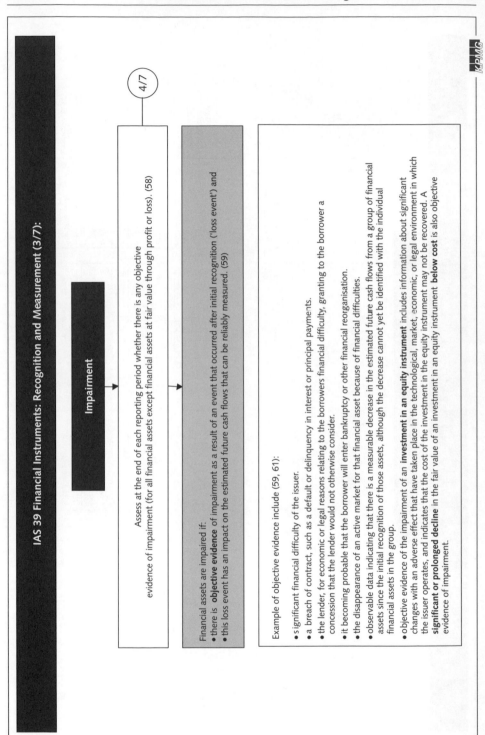

IAS 39 Financial Instruments: Recognition and Measurement (3/7):

4/7

Impairment

Assess at the end of each reporting period whether there is any objective evidence of impairment (for all financial assets except financial assets at fair value through profit or loss). (58)

Financial assets are impaired if:
- there is **objective evidence** of impairment as a result of an event that occurred after initial recognition ('loss event') and
- this loss event has an impact on the estimated future cash flows that can be reliably measured. (59)

Example of objective evidence include (59, 61):

- significant financial difficulty of the issuer.
- a breach of contract, such as a default or delinquency in interest or principal payments.
- the lender, for economic or legal reasons relating to the borrowers financial difficulty, granting to the borrower a concession that the lender would not otherwise consider.
- it becoming probable that the borrower will enter bankruptcy or other financial reorganisation.
- the disappearance of an active market for that financial asset because of financial difficulties.
- observable data indicating that there is a measurable decrease in the estimated future cash flows from a group of financial assets since the initial recognition of those assets, although the decrease cannot yet be identified with the individual financial assets in the group.
- objective evidence of the impairment of an **investment in an equity instrument** includes information about significant changes with an adverse effect that have taken place in the technological, market, economic, or legal environment in which the issuer operates, and indicates that the cost of the investment in the equity instrument may not be recovered. A **significant or prolonged decline** in the fair value of an investment in an equity instrument **below cost** is also objective evidence of impairment.

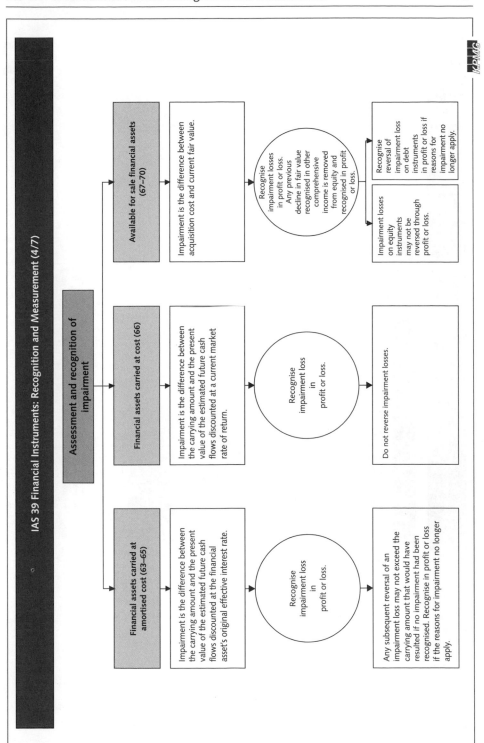

IAS 39 Financial Instruments: Recognition and Measurement (4/7)

Assessment and recognition of impairment

Financial assets carried at amortised cost (63–65)

Impairment is the difference between the carrying amount and the present value of the estimated future cash flows discounted at the financial asset's original effective interest rate.

Recognise impairment loss in profit or loss.

Any subsequent reversal of an impairment loss may not exceed the carrying amount that would have resulted if no impairment had been recognised. Recognise in profit or loss if the reasons for impairment no longer apply.

Financial assets carried at cost (66)

Impairment is the difference between the carrying amount and the present value of the estimated future cash flows discounted at a current market rate of return.

Recognise impairment loss in profit or loss.

Do not reverse impairment losses.

Available for sale financial assets (67–70)

Impairment is the difference between acquisition cost and current fair value.

Recognise impairment losses in profit or loss. Any previous decline in fair value recognised in other comprehensive income is removed from equity and recognised in profit or loss.

Impairment losses on equity instruments may not be reversed through profit or loss.

Recognise reversal of impairment loss on debt instruments in profit or loss if reasons for impairment no longer apply.

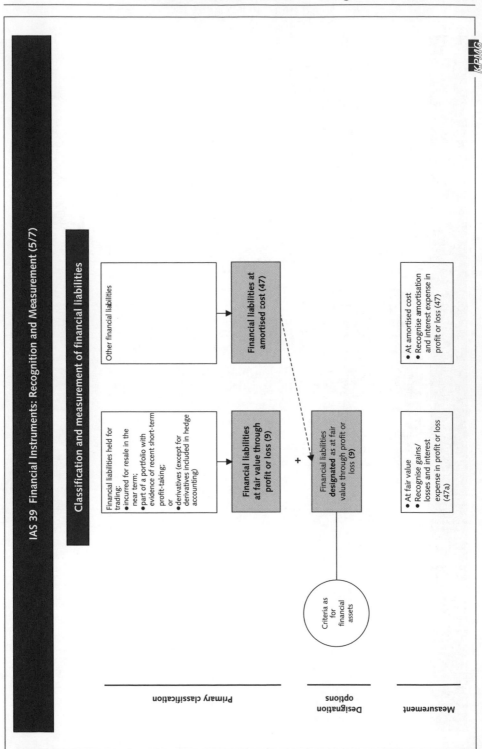

IAS 39 Financial Instruments: Recognition and Measurement (5/7)

Classification and measurement of financial liabilities

Primary classification

Financial liabilities held for trading:
- incurred for resale in the near term;
- part of a portfolio with evidence of recent short-term profit-taking; or
- derivatives (except for derivatives included in hedge accounting)

Other financial liabilities

Financial liabilities at fair value through profit or loss (9)

Financial liabilities at amortised cost (47)

Designation options

Financial liabilities **designated** as at fair value through profit or loss **(9)**

+

Criteria as for financial assets

Measurement

- At fair value
- Recognise gains/ losses and interest expense in profit or loss (47a)

- At amortised cost
- Recognise amortisation and interest expense in profit or loss (47)

KPMG

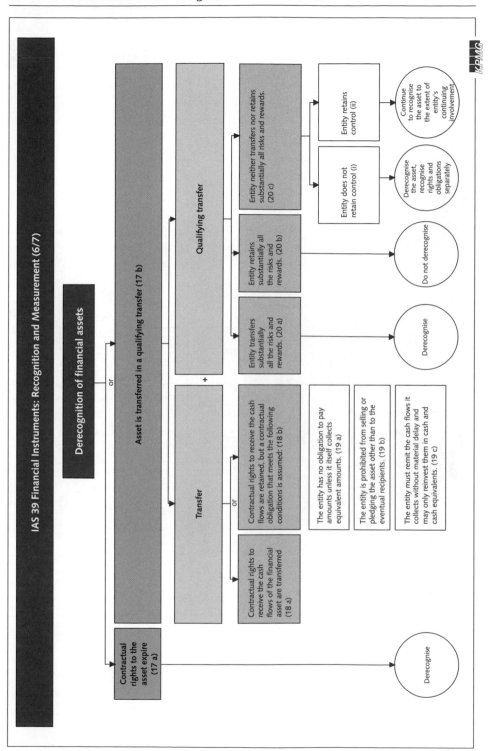

IAS 39 Financial Instruments: Recognition and Measurement (6/7)

Derecognition of financial assets

Contractual rights to the asset expire (17 a)

Asset is transferred in a qualifying transfer (17 b)

Transfer

Contractual rights to receive the cash flows of the financial asset are transferred (18 a)

Contractual rights to receive the cash flows are retained, but a contractual obligation that meets the following conditions is assumed: (18 b)

The entity has no obligation to pay amounts unless it itself collects equivalent amounts. (19 a)

The entity is prohibited from selling or pledging the asset other than to the eventual recipients. (19 b)

The entity must remit the cash flows it collects without material delay and may only reinvest them in cash and cash equivalents. (19 c)

Qualifying transfer

Entity transfers substantially all the risks and rewards. (20 a)

Entity retains substantially all the risks and rewards. (20 b)

Entity neither transfers nor retains substantially all risks and rewards. (20 c)

Entity does not retain control (i)

Entity retains control (ii)

Derecognise

Do not derecognise

Derecognise the asset, recognise rights and obligations separately

Continue to recognise the asset to the extent of entity's continuing involvement

Derecognise

IAS 39 Financial Instruments: Recognition and Measurement (7/7)

Hedging

Conditions: (88)
- Formal designation and documentation
- The hedge is expected to be highly effective (80-125%) and effectiveness is reliably measurable
- A forecast transaction must be highly probable
- The hedge is assessed on an ongoing basis and determined actually to have been highly effective throughout all periods

Consequence: Changes in fair values offset in profit or loss (85)

If the conditions are not met, recognise the derivative as a financial asset at fair value through profit or loss

Fair value hedge

Hedging instrument

Recognise gain or loss from remeasuring to fair value (or the foreign currency components measured in accordance with IAS 21) in profit or loss (89 a)

Hedged item (underlying)

The gain or loss on the hedged item attributable to the hedged risk adjusts the carrying amount of the hedged item and is recognised in profit or loss. This also generally applies if gains or losses on the hedged item are otherwise recognised in other comprehensive income. (89 b)

Cash flow hedge

Effective portion (95 a)

Recognise in other comprehensive income

Ineffective portion (95 b)

Recognise in profit or loss

Forecast transaction results in recognition of financial asset/liability (97)

Reclassify gains or losses on hedging instrument recognised in other comprehensive income from equity to profit or loss in periods during which the asset/liability affects profit or loss.

Forecast transaction results in recognition of non-financial asset/liability (98)

or

Include gains or losses on hedging instrument recognised in other comprehensive income in the initial cost of the asset/liability.

Other hedged items (100)

Reclassify gains or losses on hedging instrument recognised in other comprehensive income from equity to profit or loss in periods during which the asset/liability affects profit or loss.

Net investment in a foreign operation

Separate into effective and ineffective portions; account for them as for cash flow hedges (102)

Recognise gains or losses on the hedging instrument previously recognised in other comprehensive income in profit or loss for the period on disposal of the foreign operation. (102)

KPMG

IAS 40 Investment Property (amended 2007)

Scope:	Recognition, measurement and disclosure of investment property
Scope exclusions:	Classification and measurement of certain types of leases, biological assets, mineral rights and reserves and similar resources
Core principles:	Property (for example land, buildings) is classified as investment property if it is held to earn rentals and/or for capital appreciation, rather than for use in the production or supply of goods or services, for administrative purposes, or for sale in the ordinary course of business.
	Investment property is initially measured in the same way as property, plant and equipment. With certain exceptions, subsequent measurement of investment property uses either the cost model or the fair value model. If the fair value model is applied, property is measured at fair value and all gains and losses from changes in fair value are recognised in profit or loss.
	If an entity chooses the fair value model, property that meets the above criteria for classification as investment property that is held under an operating lease can be accounted for as if it was held under a finance lease. After capitalising the asset and recognising the corresponding liability in accordance with IAS 17, subsequent measurement uses the fair value model in accordance with IAS 40. This option can be exercised for each individual investment properties.
Effective date:	Annual periods beginning on or after 1 January 2005. Earlier application is encouraged. Amendments resulting from IAS 1 (amended 2007) must be applied at the same time as the amended IAS 1.
Applies to:	All entities

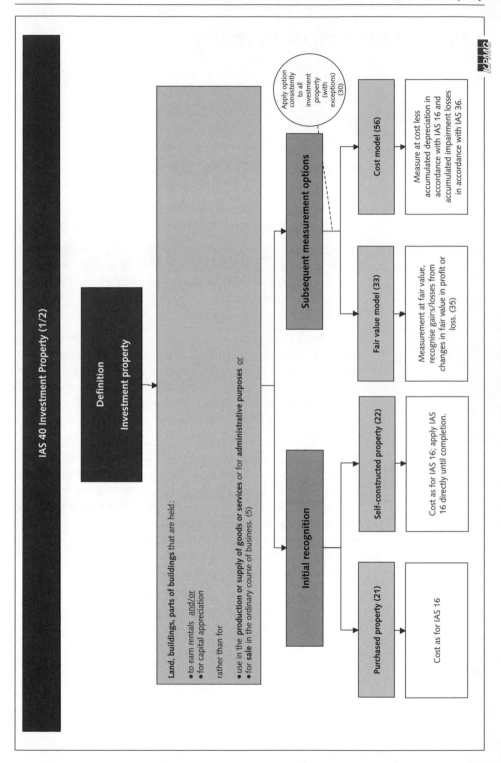

IAS 40 Investment Property (1/2)

Definition

Investment property

Land, buildings, parts of buildings that are held :

- to earn rentals and/or
- for capital appreciation

rather than for

- use in the production or supply of goods or services or for administrative purposes or
- for sale in the ordinary course of business. (5)

Initial recognition

Purchased property (21)

Cost as for IAS 16

Self-constructed property (22)

Cost as for IAS 16; apply IAS 16 directly until completion.

Subsequent measurement options

Apply option consistently to all investment property (with exceptions) (30)

Fair value model (33)

Measurement at fair value, recognise gains/losses from changes in fair value in profit or loss. (35)

Cost model (56)

Measure at cost less accumulated depreciation in accordance with IAS 16 and accumulated impairment losses in accordance with IAS 36.

KPMG

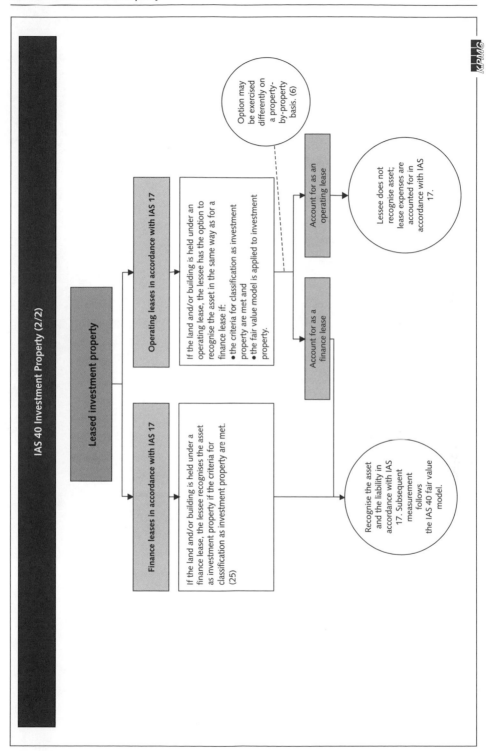

IAS 40 Investment Property (2/2)

Leased investment property

Finance leases in accordance with IAS 17

If the land and/or building is held under a finance lease, the lessee recognises the asset as investment property if the criteria for classification as investment property are met. (25)

Recognise the asset and the liability in accordance with IAS 17. Subsequent measurement follows the IAS 40 fair value model.

Operating leases in accordance with IAS 17

If the land and/or building is held under an operating lease, the lessee has the option to recognise the asset in the same way as for a finance lease if:
• the criteria for classification as investment property are met and
• the fair value model is applied to investment property.

Option may be exercised differently on a property-by-property basis. (6)

Account for as a finance lease

Account for as an operating lease

Lessee does not recognise asset; lease expenses are accounted for in accordance with IAS 17.

IAS 41 Agriculture (amended 2007)

Scope: Recognition and measurement of biological assets, agricultural produce at the point of harvest and government grants for biological assets

Scope exclusions: Land and intangible assets related to agricultural activity; agricultural products after harvest

Core principles: Biological assets are living plants and animals; agricultural produce is the harvested product of the biological assets. These assets are capitalised if the entity controls these assets as a result of past events, if it is probable that future economic benefits will flow to the entity and the fair value or the cost of the assets can be measured reliably.

Biological assets and agricultural produce at the point of harvest are measured at fair value less estimated point-of-sale costs. Any gain or loss arising on initial recognition is recognised in profit or loss. Changes in the value of biological assets are also recognised in profit or loss. After harvest, agricultural produce is accounted for as inventories in accordance with IAS 2. Fair value less estimated point-of-sale costs at the point of harvest is the cost when applying IAS 2.

Unconditional government grants related to biological assets are recognised as income when they become receivable. Conditional government grants are recognised as income only when the conditions have been met.

Effective date: Annual periods beginning on or after 1 January 2003.

Applies to: All entities

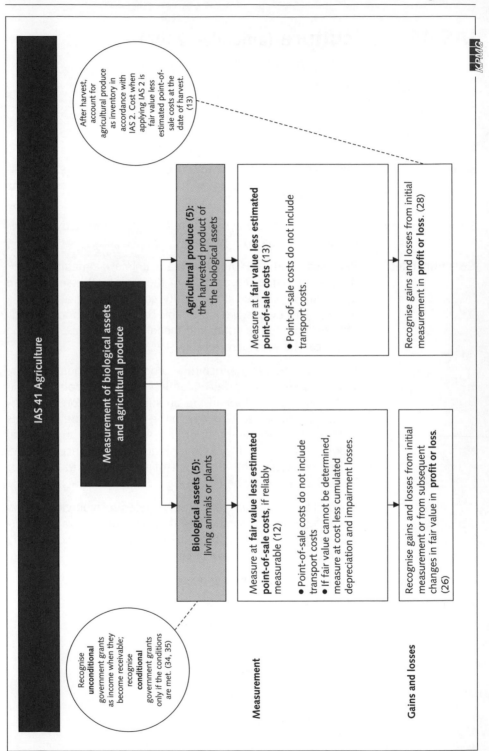

IAS 41 Agriculture

Measurement of biological assets and agricultural produce

Biological assets (5): living animals or plants

Agricultural produce (5): the harvested product of the biological assets

After harvest, account for agricultural produce as inventory in accordance with IAS 2. Cost when applying IAS 2 is fair value less estimated point-of-sale costs at the date of harvest. (13)

Recognise **unconditional** government grants as income when they become receivable; recognise **conditional** government grants only if the conditions are met. (34, 35)

Measurement

Measure at **fair value less estimated point-of-sale costs,** if reliably measurable (12)

- Point-of-sale costs do not include transport costs
- If fair value cannot be determined, measure at cost less cumulated depreciation and impairment losses.

Measure at **fair value less estimated point-of-sale costs** (13)

- Point-of-sale costs do not include transport costs.

Gains and losses

Recognise gains and losses from initial measurement or from subsequent changes in fair value in **profit or loss.** (26)

Recognise gains and losses from initial measurement in **profit or loss.** (28)

KPMG

IFRS 1 First-time Adoption of International Financial Reporting Standards
(amended 2008)

Scope:	Recognition and measurement principles for the first-time adoption of IFRSs in year-end financial statements or an interim financial report
Scope exclusions:	–
Core principles:	An entity is not a first-time adopter if its most recent financial statements contain an explicit and unreserved statement of compliance with IFRSs and it made the financial statements available to external users. All other entities are first-time adopters and must comply with the requirements of IFRS 1 when preparing IFRS financial statements.
	Entities must generally use accounting policies in their first IFRS financial statements, including for prior-period comparative figures, that comply with all IFRSs effective at the date of the first IFRS financial statements. This means that the financial statements, including prior-year comparative figures, must be presented as if IFRS had always been applied.
	In addition to this principle, IFRS 1 specifies fourteen areas for which the entity need not apply the principle, but may elect to use exemptions. The most extensive of these areas is business combinations, which are covered by detailed guidance. There are also five areas where application of the principle is prohibited.
	In addition to these recognition and measurement issues, IFRS 1 requires the presentation of reconciliations of equity and profit or loss under previous GAAP to IFRSs at various dates. Additional explanations in interim financial statements are also required.
Effective date:	Annual periods beginning on or after 1 January 2004; numerous specific requirements.
Applies to:	All entities

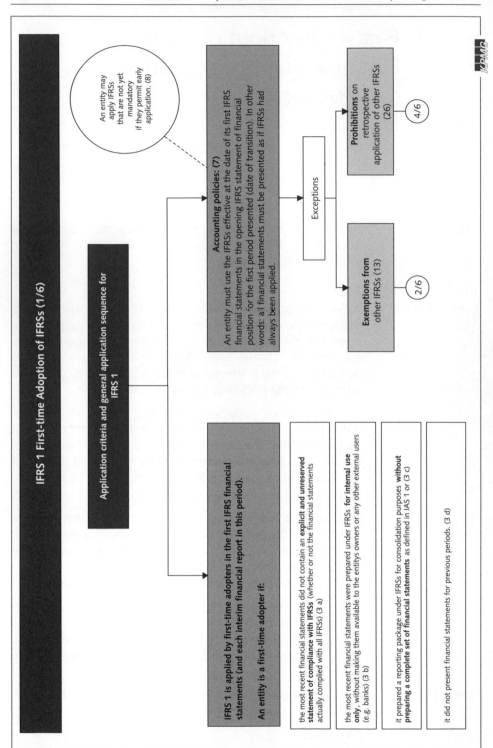

IFRS 1 First-time Adoption of IFRSs (1/6)

Application criteria and general application sequence for IFRS 1

IFRS 1 is applied by first-time adopters in the first IFRS financial statements (and each interim financial report in this period).

An entity is a first-time adopter if:

the most recent financial statements did not contain an **explicit and unreserved statement of compliance with IFRSs** (whether or not the financial statements actually complied with all IFRSs) (3 a)

the most recent financial statements were prepared under IFRSs **for internal use only**, without making them available to the entitys owners or any other external users (e.g. banks) (3 b)

it prepared a reporting package under IFRSs for consolidation purposes **without preparing a complete set of financial statements** as defined in IAS 1 or (3 c)

it did not present financial statements for previous periods. (3 d)

An entity may apply IFRSs that are not yet mandatory if they permit early application. (8)

Accounting policies: (7)
An entity must use the IFRSs effective at the date of its first IFRS financial statements in the opening IFRS statement of financial position (or the first period presented (date of transition). In other words: all financial statements must be presented as if IFRSs had always been applied.

Exceptions

Prohibitions on retrospective application of other IFRSs (26)

4/6

Exemptions from other IFRSs (13)

2/6

IFRS 1 First-time Adoption of IFRSs (2/6)

Exemptions from other IFRSs (13)

3/6

Business combinations (15)	
Fair value or revaluation as deemed cost (16-19)	Fair value measurement or revaluation of property, plant and equipment (and certain investment property and intangible assets) as deemed cost.
Employee benefits (20, 20A)	Option to recognise all cumulative actuarial gains and losses in retained earnings at the date of transition to IFRSs.
Cumulative translation differences (21, 22)	Cumulative translation differences that were previously accounted for in equity are deemed to be zero at the date of transition to IFRSs and are not included in a subsequent disposal.
Compound financial instruments (23)	Retrospective separation into liability and equity components not required if the liability component is no longer outstanding at the date of transition.
Assets and liabilities of subsidiaries, associates and joint ventures (24, 25)	Investee is first-time adopter later than parent: use carrying amounts as for parent or remeasure at investee's transition date. Parent is first-time adopter later than investee: use carrying amounts in investee's financial statements after consolidation or equity method adjustments.
Designation of previously recognised financial instruments (25A)	Independent of the classification of a financial instrument in previous GAAP financial statements, it may be redesignated at the date of transition to IFRSs.

Share-based payment transactions (25B, C)	First-time adopters are encouraged to apply IFRS 2 to legacy share-based payment transactions if it previously disclosed publicly the fair value of the equity instruments.
Insurance contracts (25D)	A first-time adopter may apply the transitional provisions of IFRS 4 instead of applying IFRS 4 in full to all periods presented.
Changes in provisions for decommissioning, etc. (25E)	No requirement to apply IFRIC 1 retrospectively. Provisions are measured under IAS 37 at date of transition, carrying amounts of assets are estimated.
Leases (25F)	No requirement to apply IFRIC 4 retrospectively. Determine whether an arrangement contains a lease at the date of transition.
Fair value measurement of financial assets/ liabilities (25G)	Certain requirements for first-time and subsequent measurement need not be applied to transactions entered into before 25 October 2002 or 1 January 2004.
Service concession arrangements (25H)	A first-time adopter may apply the transitional provisions in IFRIC 12.
Borrowing costs (25I)	A first-time adopter may apply the transitional provisions set out in IAS 23 (amended 2007).

KPMG

IFRS 1 First-time Adoption of IFRSs (3/6)

Business combinations (Appendix B)

A first-time adopter may elect not to apply IFRS 3 retrospectively to past business combinations. From the date when a first-time adopted elects to restate a business combination to comply with IFRS 3, IFRS 3 and IAS 27 (amended 2008) must also be applied to all subsequent business combinations. (B1)

If a first-time adopter does not apply IFRS 3 to a business combination, this has the following consequences for that business combination: (B2)

The first-time adopter must use the same **method** (purchase method, pooling of interests, etc.) **originally used** in its previous GAAP financial statement to account for the business combination. (a)

All assets and liabilities from the business combination must be **recognised** at the date of transition to IFRSs except:
- some financial assets and financial liabilities derecognised under previous GAAP;
- assets (including goodwill) and liabilities that were not recognised under previous GAAP and also would not qualify for recognition under IFRSs in the separate balance sheet of the acquirer;
- Any resulting change must be recognised by adjusting retained earnings unless the change results from the recognition of an intangible asset that was previously subsumed within goodwill. Such assets must be adjusted against goodwill. (b)

All assets and liabilities that do not qualify for recognition under IFRSs must be **excluded** from the opening IFRS statement of financial position. (c)

If IFRSs require **measurement at fair value**, these assets and liabilities are measured accordingly in the opening IFRS statement of financial position. Any resulting change is recognised by adjusting retained earnings. (d)

If IFRSs require **measurement at cost**, the carrying amounts at the date of the business combination are deemed cost. (e)

Assets and liabilities from a business combination that were not recognised under previous GAAP are **recognised and measured in accordance with IFRSs**. (f)

The carrying amount of **goodwill** is the carrying amount under previous GAAP at the date of transition, with only the following adjustments allowed:
- intangible assets whose accounting treatment under IFRSs differs from previous GAAP.
- Goodwill must be tested for impairment at the date of transition based on conditions at that date. (g–h)

If **goodwill** was recognised as a **deduction from equity** under previous GAAP, no goodwill is recognised in the opening IFRS statement of financial position. (i)

A **previously unconsolidated subsidiary** must be consolidated at the date of transition based on the carrying amounts of the subsidiary's assets/liabilities at that date. (j)

Non-controlling interests and **deferred tax** must be remeasured on the basis of the above adjustments to recognised assets and liabilities. (k)

The exemptions also apply to past acquisitions of investments in associates and joint ventures (B3)

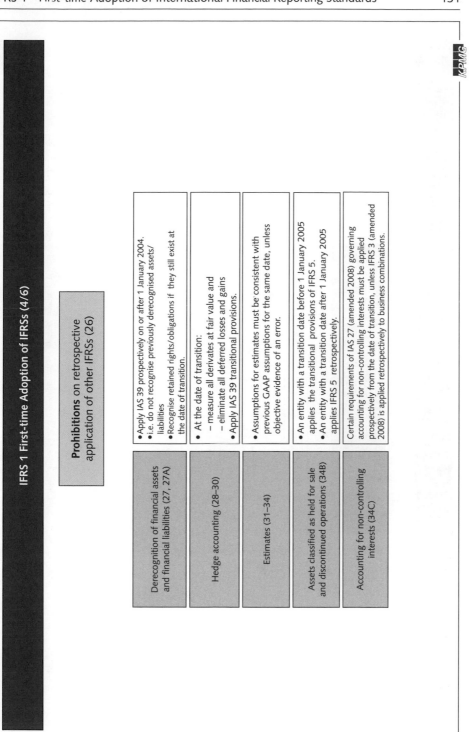

IFRS 1 First-time Adoption of IFRSs (4/6)

Prohibitions on retrospective application of other IFRSs (26)

Derecognition of financial assets and financial liabilities (27, 27A)	• Apply IAS 39 prospectively on or after 1 January 2004. • i.e. do not recognise previously derecognised assets/liabilities • Recognise retained rights/obligations if they still exist at the date of transition.
Hedge accounting (28–30)	• At the date of transition: – measure all derivates at fair value and – eliminate all deferred losses and gains • Apply IAS 39 transitional provisions.
Estimates (31–34)	• Assumptions for estimates must be consistent with previous GAAP assumptions for the same date, unless objective evidence of an error.
Assets classified as held for sale and discontinued operations (34B)	• An entity with a transition date before 1 January 2005 applies the transitional provisions of IFRS 5. • An entity with a transition date after 1 January 2005 applies IFRS 5 retrospectively.
Accounting for non-controlling interests (34C)	Certain requirements of IAS 27 (amended 2008) governing accounting for non-controlling interests must be applied prospectively from the date of transition, unless IFRS 3 (amended 2008) is applied retrospectively to business combinations.

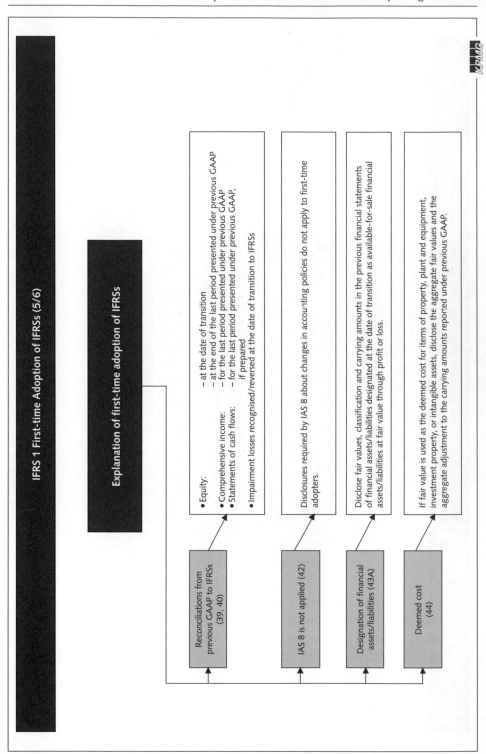

IFRS 1 First-time Adoption of IFRSs (5/6)

Explanation of first-time adoption of IFRSs

Reconciliations from previous GAAP to IFRSs (39, 40)

- Equity:
  - at the date of transition
  - at the end of the last period presented under previous GAAP
- Comprehensive income:
  - for the last period presented under previous GAAP
- Statements of cash flows:
  - for the last period presented under previous GAAP, if prepared
- Impairment losses recognised/reversed at the date of transition to IFRSs

IAS 8 is not applied (42)

Disclosures required by IAS 8 about changes in accounting policies do not apply to first-time adopters.

Designation of financial assets/liabilities (43A)

Disclose fair values, classification and carrying amounts in the previous financial statements of financial assets/liabilities designated at the date of transition as available-for-sale financial assets/liabilities at fair value through profit or loss.

Deemed cost (44)

If fair value is used as the deemed cost for items of property, plant and equipment, investment property, or intangible assets, disclose the aggregate fair values and the aggregate adjustment to the carrying amounts reported under previous GAAP.

KPMG

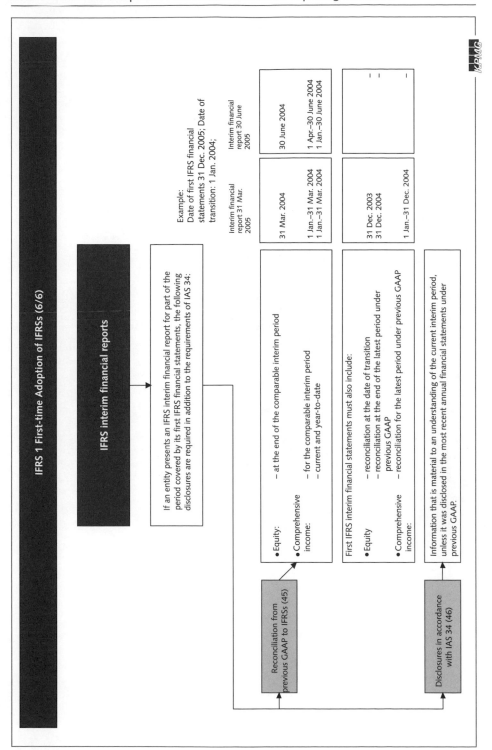

IFRS 1 First-time Adoption of IFRSs (6/6)

IFRS interim financial reports

If an entity presents an IFRS interim financial report for part of the period covered by its first IFRS financial statements, the following disclosures are required in addition to the requirements of IAS 34:

Reconciliation from previous GAAP to IFRSs (45)

- Equity:
  - at the end of the comparable interim period
- Comprehensive income:
  - for the comparable interim period
  - current and year-to-date

First IFRS interim financial statements must also include:

- Equity:
  - reconciliation at the date of transition
  - reconciliation at the end of the latest period under previous GAAP
- Comprehensive income:
  - reconciliation for the latest period under previous GAAP

Disclosures in accordance with IAS 34 (46)

Information that is material to an understanding of the current interim period, unless it was disclosed in the most recent annual financial statements under previous GAAP.

Example:
Date of first IFRS financial statements 31 Dec. 2005; Date of transition: 1 Jan. 2004;

	Interim financial report 31 Mar. 2005	Interim financial report 30 June 2005
	31 Mar. 2004	30 June 2004
	1 Jan.–31 Mar. 2004	1 Apr.–30 June 2004
	1 Jan.–31 Mar. 2004	1 Jan.–30 June 2004
	31 Dec. 2003	– –
	31 Dec. 2004	
	1 Jan.–31 Dec. 2004	–

IFRS 2 Share-based Payment (amended 2008)

Scope:	Accounting for share-based payment transactions
Scope exclusions:	Share-based payments as part of business combinations; share-based payments for the acquisition of certain financial instruments.
Core principles:	In share-based payment transactions, an entity receives goods or services and grants equity instruments (equity-settled share-based payment transactions) or incurs a liability (cash-settled share-based payment transactions) as consideration. The liability is settled either in cash or other assets. For accounting purposes, share-based payment transactions are classified into three categories:
	Equity-settled share-based payment transactions are generally measured at the fair value of the goods or services received (direct measurement). If fair value cannot be measured reliably, the goods and services received are measured at the fair value of the equity instruments granted (indirect measurement). This is always the case for services received from employees.
	Cash-settled share-based payment transactions are measured at the fair value of the liability. Any changes in fair value are recognised in profit or loss at the end of each reporting period.
	Depending on the contractual terms, share-based payment transactions with cash alternatives (settlement in equity instruments, cash, or other assets) are either recognised in full as equity-settled or cash-settled transactions, or the components are split into the two categories.
Effective date:	Annual periods beginning on or after 1 January 2005. Earlier application is encouraged.
Applies to:	All entities

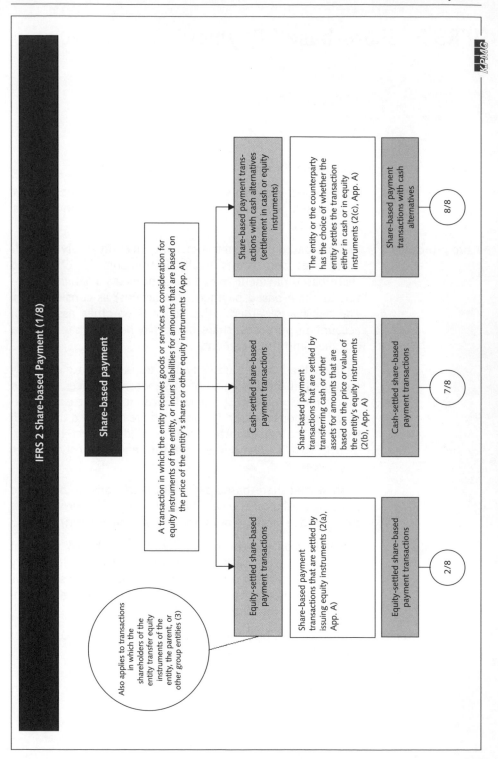

IFRS 2 Share-based Payment (1/8)

Share-based payment

A transaction in which the entity receives goods or services as consideration for equity instruments of the entity, or incurs liabilities for amounts that are based on the price of the entity's shares or other equity instruments (App. A)

Also applies to transactions in which the shareholders of the entity transfer equity instruments of the entity, the parent, or other group entities (3)

Equity-settled share-based payment transactions

Share-based payment transactions that are settled by issuing equity instruments (2(a), App. A)

Equity-settled share-based payment transactions

2/8

Cash-settled share-based payment transactions

Share-based payment transactions that are settled by transferring cash or other assets for amounts that are based on the price or value of the entity's equity instruments (2(b), App. A)

Cash-settled share-based payment transactions

7/8

Share-based payment trans-actions with cash alternatives (settlement in cash or equity instruments)

The entity or the counterparty has the choice of whether the entity settles the transaction either in cash or in equity instruments (2(c), App. A)

Share-based payment transactions with cash alternatives

8/8

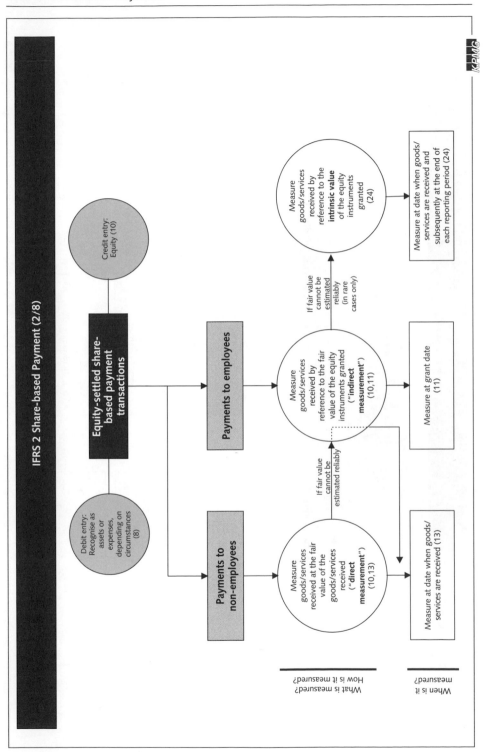

IFRS 2 Share-based Payment (2/8)

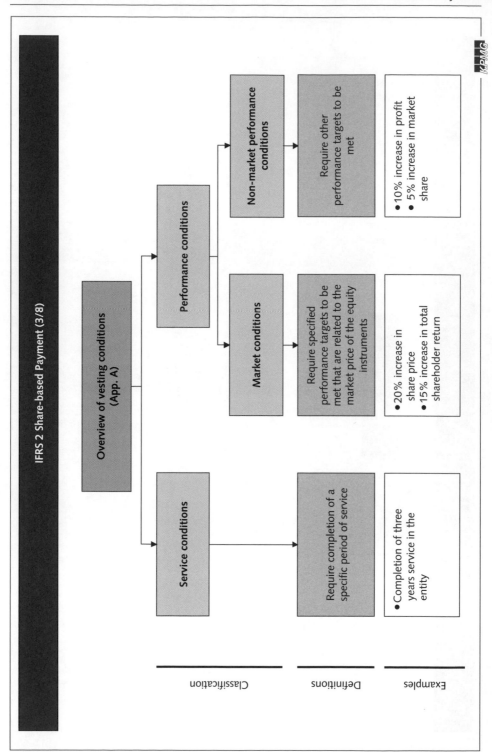

IFRS 2 Share-based Payment (3/8)

Overview of vesting conditions (App. A)

Service conditions

Performance conditions

Market conditions

Non-market performance conditions

Require completion of a specific period of service

Require specified performance targets to be met that are related to the market price of the equity instruments

Require other performance targets to be met

- Completion of three years service in the entity

- 20% increase in share price
- 15% increase in total shareholder return

- 10% increase in profit
- 5% increase in market share

Classification

Definitions

Examples

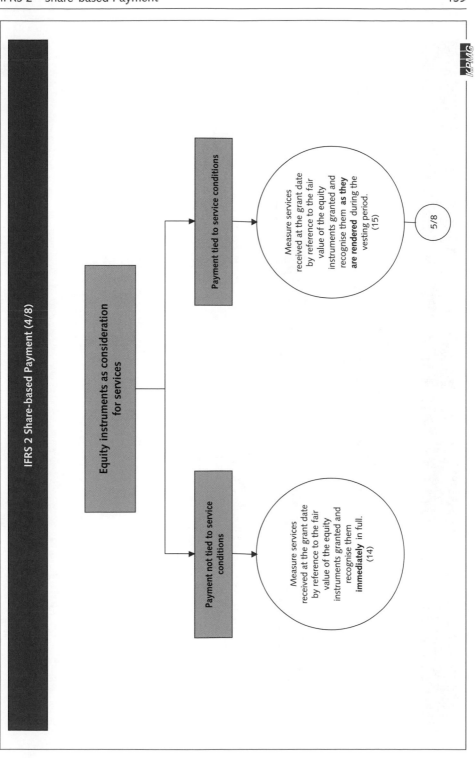

IFRS 2 Share-based Payment (4/8)

Equity instruments as consideration for services

Payment not tied to service conditions

Measure services received at the grant date by reference to the fair value of the equity instruments granted and recognise them **immediately** in full. (14)

Payment tied to service conditions

Measure services received at the grant date by reference to the fair value of the equity instruments granted and recognise them **as they are rendered** during the vesting period. (15)

5/8

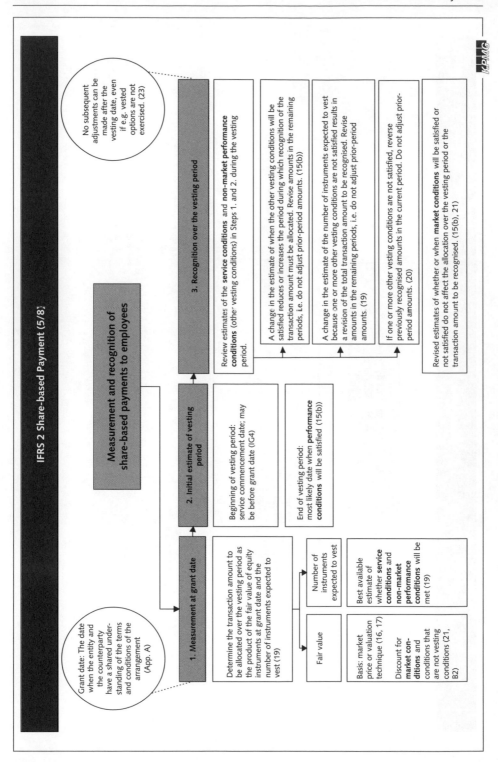

IFRS 2 Share-based Payment (5/8)

Measurement and recognition of share-based payments to employees

No subsequent adjustments can be made after the vesting date, even if e.g. vested options are not exercised. (23)

Grant date: The date when the entity and the counterparty have a shared understanding of the terms and conditions of the arrangement (App. A)

1. Measurement at grant date

Determine the transaction amount to be allocated over the vesting period as the product of the fair value of equity instruments at grant date and the number of instruments expected to vest (19)

Fair value

Number of instruments expected to vest

Basis: market price or valuation technique (16, 17)

Discount for **market conditions** and conditions that are not vesting conditions (21, B2)

Best available estimate of whether **service conditions** and **non-market performance conditions** will be met (19)

2. Initial estimate of vesting period

Beginning of vesting period: service commencement date; may be before grant date (IG4)

End of vesting period: most likely date when **performance conditions** will be satisfied (15(b))

3. Recognition over the vesting period

Review estimates of the **service conditions** and **non-market performance conditions** (other vesting conditions) in Steps 1. and 2. during the vesting period.

A change in the estimate of when the other vesting conditions will be satisfied reduces or increases the period during which recognition of the transaction amount must be allocated. Revise amounts in the remaining periods, i.e. do not adjust prior-period amounts. (15(b))

A change in the estimate of the number of instruments expected to vest because one or more other vesting conditions are not satisfied results in a revision of the total transaction amount to be recognised. Revise amounts in the remaining periods, i.e. do not adjust prior-period amounts. (19)

If one or more other vesting conditions are not satisfied, reverse previously recognised amounts in the current period. Do not adjust prior-period amounts. (20)

Revised estimates of whether or when **market conditions** will be satisfied or not satisfied do not affect the allocation over the vesting period or the transaction amount to be recognised. (15(b), 21)

KPMG

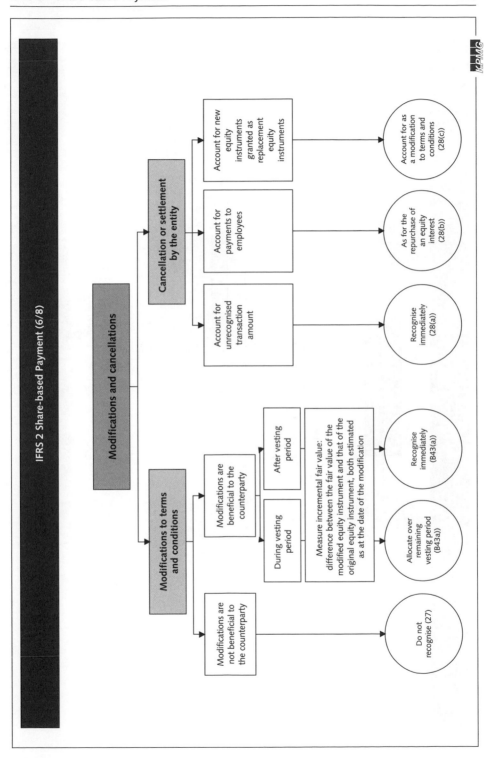

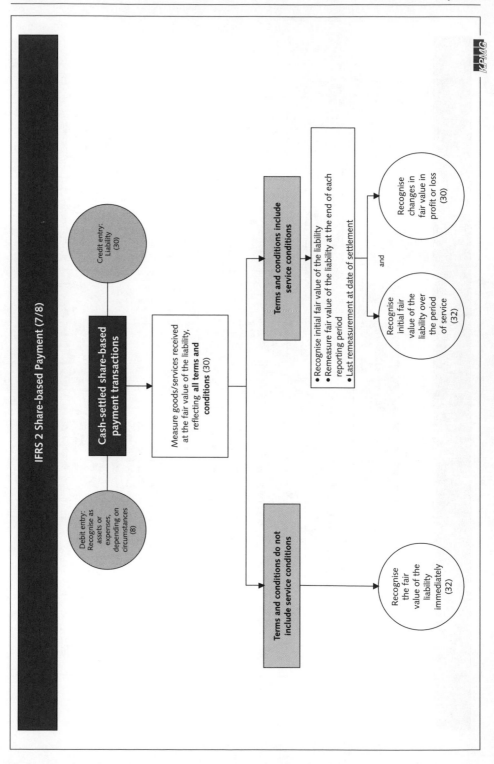

IFRS 2 Share-based Payment (7/8)

Debit entry: Recognise as assets or expenses, depending on circumstances (8)

Cash-settled share-based payment transactions

Credit entry: Liability (30)

Measure goods/services received at the fair value of the liability, reflecting all terms and conditions (30)

Terms and conditions do not include service conditions

Terms and conditions include service conditions

Recognise the fair value of the liability immediately (32)

- Recognise initial fair value of the liability
- Remeasure fair value of the liability at the end of each reporting period
- Last remeasurement at date of settlement

Recognise initial fair value of the liability over the period of service (32)

and

Recognise changes in fair value in profit or loss (30)

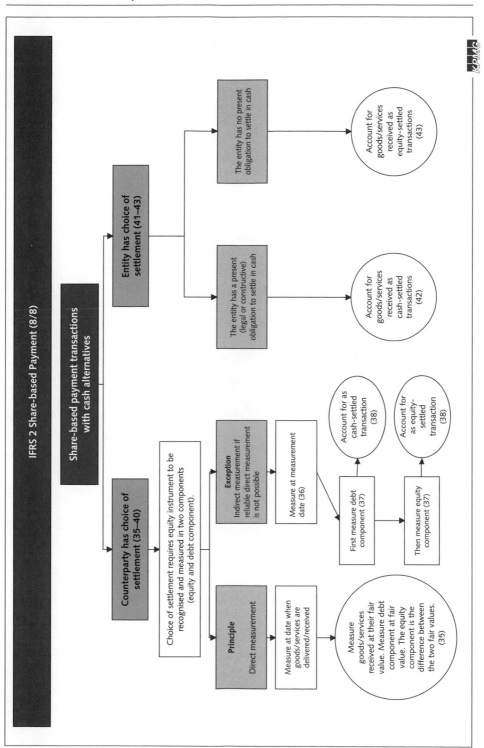

IFRS 3 Business Combinations
(amended 2008)

Scope:	Accounting for business combinations
Scope exclusions:	Formation of joint ventures, acquisition of assets that do not constitute a business as defined in the Standard, common control transactions
Core principles:	A business combination is a transaction or other event in which an acquirer obtains control of one or more businesses.
	At the acquisition date, the acquirer recognises all identifiable assets acquired and liabilities assumed and measures them at fair value; there are exceptions for certain assets and liabilities. Any non-controlling interest is measured either at fair value or at the non-controlling interest's proportionate share of the acquiree's identifiable net assets.
	The consideration transferred consists of assets transferred, liabilities incurred, equity interests issued and contingent consideration, all of which are measured at their acquisition-date fair values.
	The excess of the consideration transferred, plus the amount of any non-controlling interest, over the acquiree's identifiable net assets is recognised as goodwill. If the excess is negative, the acquirer recognises a gain from a bargain purchase.
Effective date:	Business combinations for which the acquisition date is in financial years beginning on or after 1 July 2009; earlier application for financial years beginning on or after 30 June 2007 is permitted, provided that IAS 27 (amended 2008) is applied at the same time. IFRS 3 (2004) must be applied before this time.
Applies to:	All entities

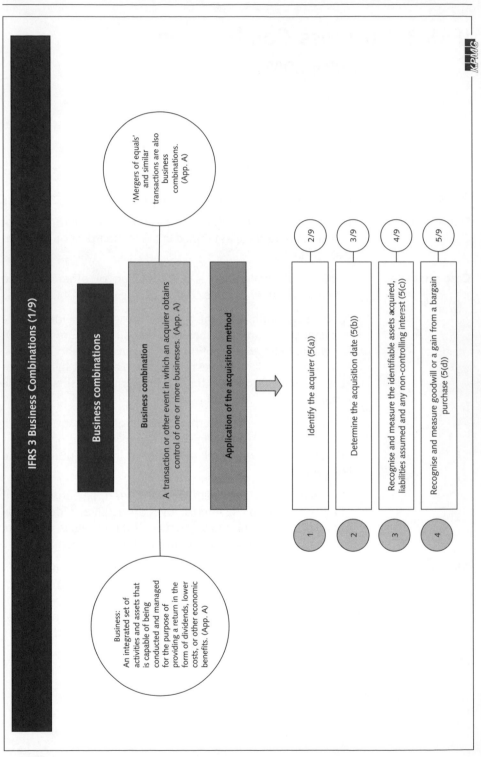

IFRS 3 Business Combinations (1/9)

Business combinations

Business combination

A transaction or other event in which an acquirer obtains control of one or more businesses. (App. A)

'Mergers of equals' and similar transactions are also business combinations. (App. A)

Business:
An integrated set of activities and assets that is capable of being conducted and managed for the purpose of providing a return in the form of dividends, lower costs, or other economic benefits. (App. A)

Application of the acquisition method

1 Identify the acquirer (5(a))   2/9

2 Determine the acquisition date (5(b))   3/9

3 Recognise and measure the identifiable assets acquired, liabilities assumed and any non-controlling interest (5(c))   4/9

4 Recognise and measure goodwill or a gain from a bargain purchase (5(d))   5/9

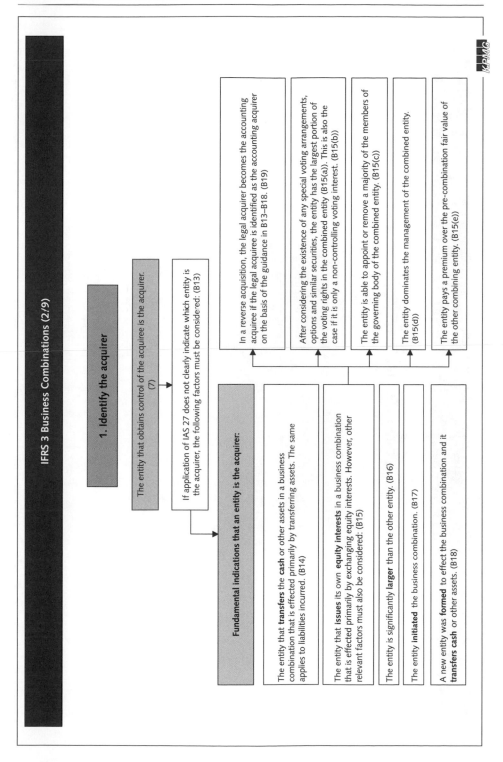

IFRS 3 Business Combinations (2/9)

1. Identify the acquirer

The entity that obtains control of the acquiree is the acquirer. (7)

If application of IAS 27 does not clearly indicate which entity is the acquirer, the following factors must be considered: (B13)

Fundamental indications that an entity is the acquirer:

The entity that **transfers** the **cash** or other assets in a business combination that is effected primarily by transferring assets. The same applies to liabilities incurred. (B14)

The entity that **issues** its own **equity interests** in a business combination that is effected primarily by exchanging equity interests. However, other relevant factors must also be considered: (B15)

The entity is significantly **larger** than the other entity. (B16)

The entity **initiated** the business combination. (B17)

A new entity was **formed** to effect the business combination and it **transfers cash** or other assets. (B18)

In a reverse acquisition, the legal acquirer becomes the accounting acquiree if the legal acquirer is identified as the accounting acquirer on the basis of the guidance in B13–B18. (B19)

After considering the existence of any special voting arrangements, options and similar securities, the entity has the largest portion of the voting rights in the combined entity (B15(a)). This is also the case if it is only a non-controlling voting interest. (B15(b))

The entity is able to appoint or remove a majority of the members of the governing body of the combined entity. (B15(c))

The entity dominates the management of the combined entity. (B15(d))

The entity pays a premium over the pre-combination fair value of the other combining entity. (B15(e))

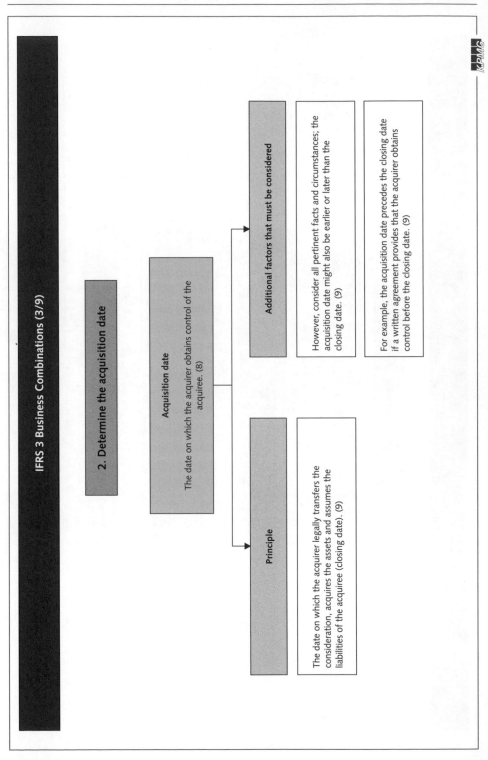

IFRS 3 Business Combinations (3/9)

2. Determine the acquisition date

Acquisition date

The date on which the acquirer obtains control of the acquiree. (8)

Principle

The date on which the acquirer legally transfers the consideration, acquires the assets and assumes the liabilities of the acquiree (closing date). (9)

Additional factors that must be considered

However, consider all pertinent facts and circumstances; the acquisition date might also be earlier or later than the closing date. (9)

For example, the acquisition date precedes the closing date if a written agreement provides that the acquirer obtains control before the closing date. (9)

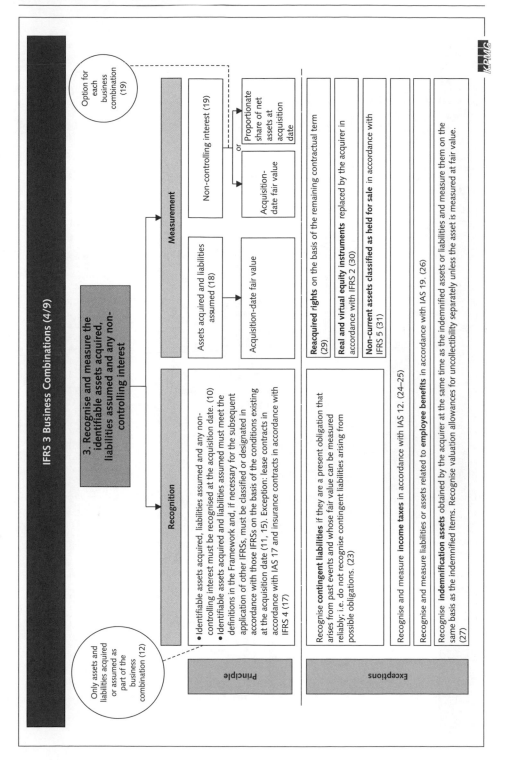

IFRS 3 Business Combinations (4/9)

Option for each business combination (19)

Only assets and liabilities acquired or assumed as part of the business combination (12)

3. Recognise and measure the identifiable assets acquired, liabilities assumed and any non-controlling interest

Recognition

Measurement

Non-controlling interest (19)

Proportionate share of net assets at acquisition date

or

Acquisition-date fair value

Assets acquired and liabilities assumed (18)

Acquisition-date fair value

Principle

- Identifiable assets acquired, liabilities assumed and any non-controlling interest must be recognised at the acquisition date. (10)
- Identifiable assets acquired and liabilities assumed must meet the definitions in the Framework and, if necessary for the subsequent application of other IFRSs, must be classified or designated in accordance with those IFRSs on the basis of the conditions existing at the acquisition date (11, 15). Exception: lease contracts in accordance with IAS 17 and insurance contracts in accordance with IFRS 4 (17)

Exceptions

Recognise **contingent liabilities** if they are a present obligation that arises from past events and whose fair value can be measured reliably; i.e. do not recognise contingent liabilities arising from possible obligations. (23)

Recognise and measure **income taxes** in accordance with IAS 12. (24–25)

Recognise and measure liabilities or assets related to **employee benefits** in accordance with IAS 19. (26)

Recognise **indemnification assets** obtained by the acquirer at the same time as the indemnified assets or liabilities and measure them on the same basis as the indemnified items. Recognise valuation allowances for uncollectibility separately unless the asset is measured at fair value. (27)

Reacquired rights on the basis of the remaining contractual term (29)

Real and virtual equity instruments replaced by the acquirer in accordance with IFRS 2 (30)

Non-current assets classified as held for sale in accordance with IFRS 5 (31)

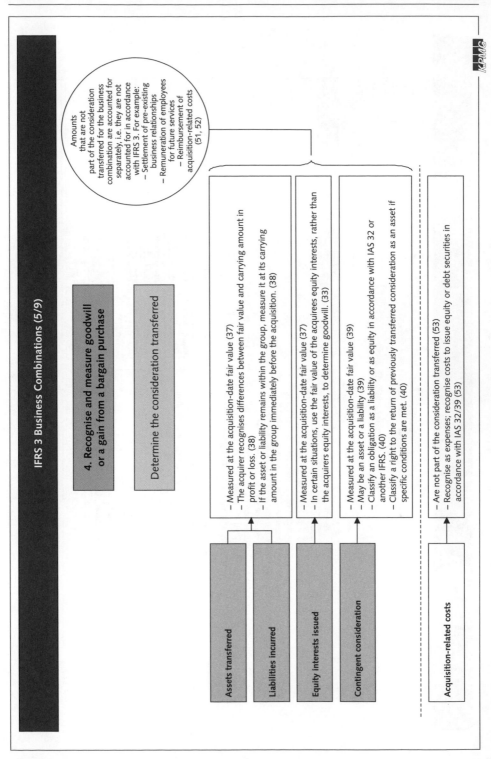

IFRS 3 Business Combinations (5/9)

4. Recognise and measure goodwill or a gain from a bargain purchase

Determine the consideration transferred

Amounts that are not part of the consideration transferred for the business combination are accounted for separately, i.e. they are not accounted for in accordance with IFRS 3. For example:
– Settlement of pre-existing business relationships
– Remuneration of employees for future services
– Reimbursement of acquisition-related costs (51, 52)

Assets transferred
– Measured at the acquisition-date fair value (37)
– The acquirer recognises differences between fair value and carrying amount in profit or loss. (38)

Liabilities incurred
– If the asset or liability remains within the group, measure it at its carrying amount in the group immediately before the acquisition. (38)

Equity interests issued
– Measured at the acquisition-date fair value (37)
– In certain situations, use the fair value of the acquirees equity interests, rather than the acquirers equity interests, to determine goodwill. (33)

Contingent consideration
– Measured at the acquisition-date fair value (39)
– May be an asset or a liability (39)
– Classify an obligation as a liability or as equity in accordance with IAS 32 or another IFRS. (40)
– Classify a right to the return of previously transferred consideration as an asset if specific conditions are met. (40)

Acquisition-related costs
– Are not part of the consideration transferred (53)
– Recognise as expenses; recognise costs to issue equity or debt securities in accordance with IAS 32/39 (53)

KPMG

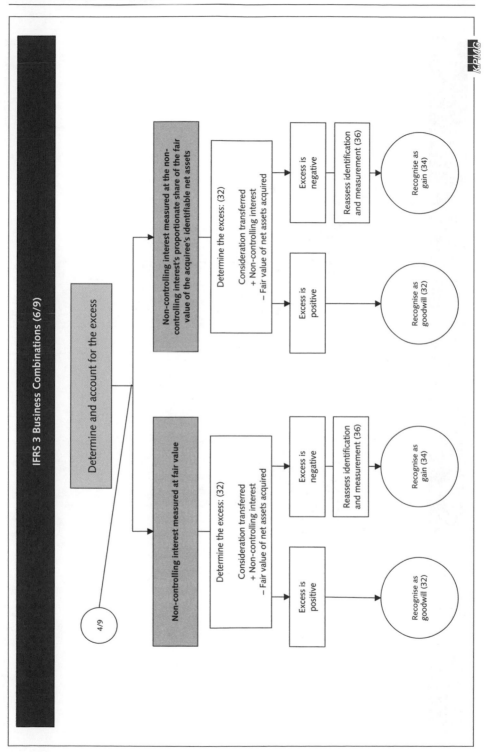

IFRS 3 Business Combinations (6/9)

Determine and account for the excess

4/9

Non-controlling interest measured at fair value

Determine the excess: (32)

Consideration transferred
+ Non-controlling interest
– Fair value of net assets acquired

Excess is positive

Excess is negative

Reassess identification and measurement (36)

Recognise as goodwill (32)

Recognise as gain (34)

Non-controlling interest measured at the non-controlling interest's proportionate share of the fair value of the acquiree's identifiable net assets

Determine the excess: (32)

Consideration transferred
+ Non-controlling interest
– Fair value of net assets acquired

Excess is positive

Excess is negative

Reassess identification and measurement (36)

Recognise as goodwill (32)

Recognise as gain (34)

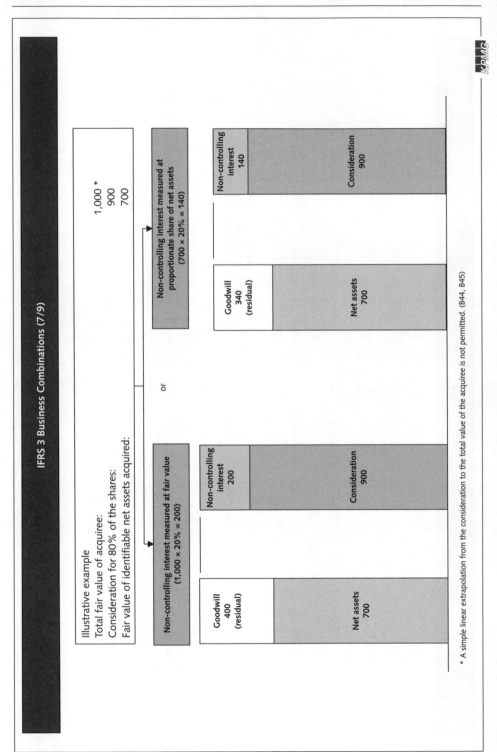

IFRS 3 Business Combinations (7/9)

Illustrative example
Total fair value of acquiree: 1,000 *
Consideration for 80% of the shares: 900
Fair value of identifiable net assets acquired: 700

Non-controlling interest measured at fair value
(1,000 × 20% = 200)

or

Non-controlling interest measured at
proportionate share of net assets
(700 × 20% = 140)

Goodwill
400
(residual)

Non-controlling
interest
200

Net assets
700

Consideration
900

Goodwill
340
(residual)

Non-controlling
interest
140

Net assets
700

Consideration
900

* A simple linear extrapolation from the consideration to the total value of the acquiree is not permitted. (B44, B45)

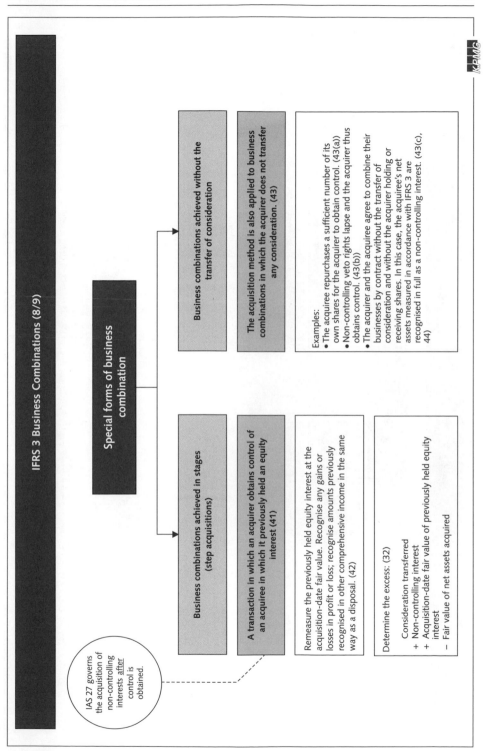

IFRS 3 Business Combinations (8/9)

Special forms of business combination

IAS 27 governs the acquisition of non-controlling interests *after* control is obtained.

Business combinations achieved in stages (step acquisitions)

A transaction in which an acquirer obtains control of an acquiree in which it previously held an equity interest (41)

Remeasure the previously held equity interest at the acquisition-date fair value. Recognise any gains or losses in profit or loss; recognise amounts previously recognised in other comprehensive income in the same way as a disposal. (42)

Determine the excess: (32)

  Consideration transferred
+ Non-controlling interest
+ Acquisition-date fair value of previously held equity interest
− Fair value of net assets acquired

Business combinations achieved without the transfer of consideration

The acquisition method is also applied to business combinations in which the acquirer does not transfer any consideration. (43)

Examples:
● The acquiree repurchases a sufficient number of its own shares for the acquirer to obtain control. (43(a))
● Non-controlling veto rights lapse and the acquirer thus obtains control. (43(b))
● The acquirer and the acquiree agree to combine their businesses by contract without the transfer of consideration and without the acquirer holding or receiving shares. In this case, the acquiree's net assets measured in accordance with IFRS 3 are recognised in full as a non-controlling interest. (43(c), 44)

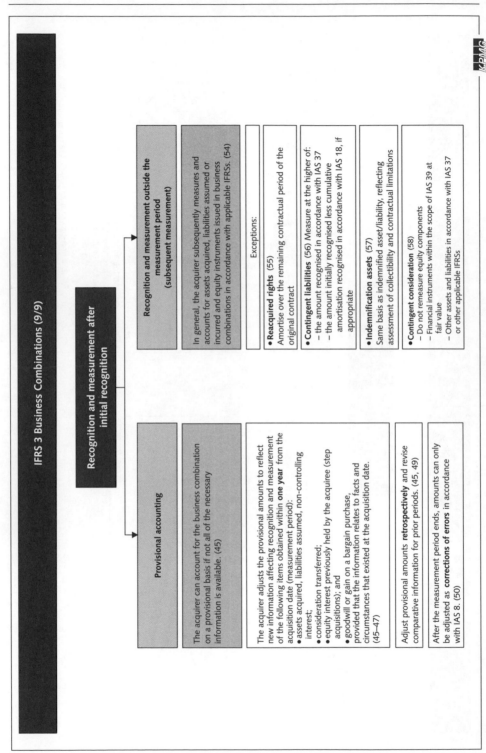

IFRS 3 Business Combinations (9/9)

Recognition and measurement after initial recognition

Provisional accounting

The acquirer can account for the business combination on a provisional basis if not all of the necessary information is available. (45)

The acquirer adjusts the provisional amounts to reflect new information affecting recognition and measurement of the following items obtained within **one year** from the acquisition date (measurement period):
- assets acquired, liabilities assumed, non-controlling interest;
- consideration transferred;
- equity interest previously held by the acquiree (step acquisitions); and
- goodwill or gain on a bargain purchase,

provided that the information relates to facts and circumstances that existed at the acquisition date. (45–47)

Adjust provisional amounts **retrospectively** and revise comparative information for prior periods. (45, 49)

After the measurement period ends, amounts can only be adjusted as **corrections of errors** in accordance with IAS 8. (50)

Recognition and measurement outside the measurement period (subsequent measurement)

In general, the acquirer subsequently measures and accounts for assets acquired, liabilities assumed or incurred and equity instruments issued in business combinations in accordance with applicable IFRSs. (54)

Exceptions:

- **Reacquired rights** (55)
  Amortise over the remaining contractual period of the original contract

- **Contingent liabilities** (56) Measure at the higher of:
  - the amount recognised in accordance with IAS 37
  - the amount initially recognised less cumulative amortisation recognised in accordance with IAS 18, if appropriate

- **Indemnification assets** (57)
  Same basis as indemnified asset/liability, reflecting assessment of collectibility and contractual limitations

- **Contingent consideration** (58)
  - Do not remeasure equity components
  - Financial instruments within the scope of IAS 39 at fair value
  - Other assets and liabilities in accordance with IAS 37 or other applicable IFRSs

IFRS 4 Insurance Contracts (amended 2007)

Scope:	Accounting for insurance contracts that an entity issues, reinsurance contracts that it holds and financial instruments that it issues with a discretionary participation feature. IFRS 4 does not only apply to entities that are regarded as insurers for regulatory purposes.
Scope exemptions:	Financial instruments within the scope of IAS 32 or IAS 39, as long as they do not contain a discretionary participation feature; product warranties; employers' obligations under employee benefit plans; contractual rights or obligations that are contingent on the future use of non-financial items; certain financial guarantees; contingent consideration payable or receivable in a business combination; direct insurance contracts held by the entity.
Core principles:	Insurance contracts and – with certain additional restrictions – financial instruments with a discretionary participation feature must be recognised and measured in accordance with certain fundamental considerations. In particular, recognised insurance liabilities must be adequate and reinsurance assets must be tested for impairment. Any embedded derivatives and financial components must be separated. Apart from these principles, entities must continue to apply the accounting policies applied before the introduction of IFRS 4. Changes in existing accounting policies may only be made if they enhance the relevance of the financial statements without impairing reliability, or enhance reliability without impairing relevance.
Effective date	Annual periods beginning on or after 1 January 2005. Earlier application is encouraged. Amendments resulting from IAS 1 (amended 2007) must be applied at the same time as the amended IAS 1.
Applies to:	All entities

IFRS 4 Insurance Contracts (1/3)

Insurance contracts

An insurance contract is a contract under which one party (the insurer) accepts significant insurance risk from another party (the policyholder) by agreeing to compensate the policyholder if a specified uncertain future event (the insured event) adversely affects the policy holder. (App. A)

Insurance risk (Appendix A)

Risk, other than financial risk, transferred from the holder of a contract to the issuer.

Financial risk is the risk of a possible future change in interest rates, financial instrument prices, commodity prices, exchange rates, indices of prices or rates, credit ratings, or other variables. Non-financial variables are included if they are not specific to a contracting party.

Significance (App. B, B 22–28)

Insurance risk is significant if an insured event that has commercial substance could cause an insurer to pay significant additional benefits.

Additional benefits are amounts (including the costs of handling and assessing claims) that exceed those that would be payable if no insured event occurred.

There is no commercial substance if the probability that the insured event will occur does not affect business decisions or the economics of a transaction, i.e. no higher price would be paid for insurance cover.

Uncertain future event (App. B, B 2–4)

Uncertainty is the essence of an insurance contract and relates to at least one of the following characteristics:
• uncertainty about whether an insured event will occur
• uncertainty about when it will occur
• uncertainty about how much the insurer will need to pay if it occurs.

KPMG

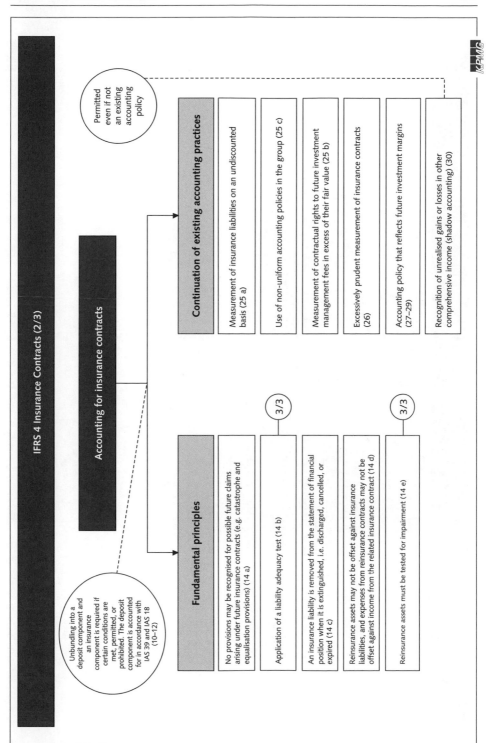

IFRS 4 Insurance Contracts (2/3)

Accounting for insurance contracts

Unbundling into a deposit component and an insurance component is required if certain conditions are met, permitted, or prohibited. The deposit component is accounted for in accordance with IAS 39 and IAS 18 (10–12)

Permitted even if not an existing accounting policy

Fundamental principles

No provisions may be recognised for possible future claims arising under future insurance contracts (e.g. catastrophe and equalisation provisions) (14 a)

Application of a liability adequacy test (14 b)

3/3

An insurance liability is removed from the statement of financial position when it is extinguished, i.e. discharged, cancelled, or expired (14 c)

Reinsurance assets may not be offset against insurance liabilities, and expenses from reinsurance contracts may not be offset against income from the related insurance contract (14 d)

3/3

Reinsurance assets must be tested for impairment (14 e)

Continuation of existing accounting practices

Measurement of insurance liabilities on an undiscounted basis (25 a)

Use of non-uniform accounting policies in the group (25 c)

Measurement of contractual rights to future investment management fees in excess of their fair value (25 b)

Excessively prudent measurement of insurance contracts (26)

Accounting policy that reflects future investment margins (27–29)

Recognition of unrealised gains or losses in other comprehensive income (shadow accounting) (30)

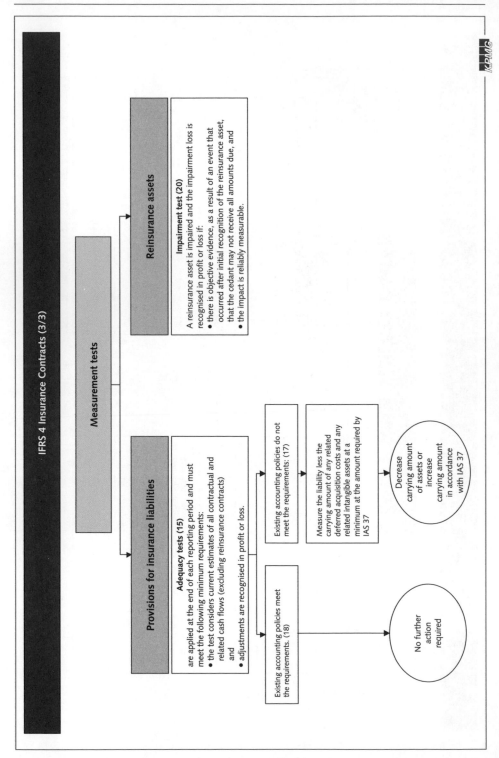

IFRS 4 Insurance Contracts (3/3)

Measurement tests

Reinsurance assets

Impairment test (20)
A reinsurance asset is impaired and the impairment loss is recognised in profit or loss if:
• there is objective evidence, as a result of an event that occurred after initial recognition of the reinsurance asset, that the cedant may not receive all amounts due, and
• the impact is reliably measurable.

Provisions for insurance liabilities

Adequacy tests (15)
are applied at the end of each reporting period and must meet the following minimum requirements:
• the test considers current estimates of all contractual and related cash flows (excluding reinsurance contracts) and
• adjustments are recognised in profit or loss.

Existing accounting policies do not meet the requirements: (17)

Measure the liability less the carrying amount of any related deferred acquisition costs and any related intangible assets at a minimum at the amount required by IAS 37

Decrease carrying amount of assets or increase carrying amount in accordance with IAS 37

Existing accounting policies meet the requirements. (18)

No further action required

IFRS 5 Non-current Assets Held for Sale and Discontinued Operations

(amended 2008)

Scope:	Measurement, presentation and disclosure of non-current assets and disposal groups held for sale, and the presentation and disclosure of discontinued operations
Scope exclusions:	The measurement provisions do not apply to deferred tax assets, assets arising from employee benefits, financial assets within the scope of IAS 39, investment property accounted for using the fair value model, biological assets accounted for at fair value less estimated point-of-sale costs, and contractual rights under insurance contracts.
Core principles:	Non-current assets held for sale are available for immediate sale. Their sale must be highly probable, i.e. certain objective features indicate that the sale process is at an advanced stage. Immediately before classification as held for sale, the current carrying amount must be measured in accordance with applicable IFRSs. The assets are then measured at the lower of their carrying amount and fair value less costs to sell. Depreciation or amortisation of non-current assets held for sale is discontinued. The assets are presented separately in the statement of financial position. Special requirements apply to groups of assets and liabilities that will be sold together (disposal groups).
	Discontinued operations are clearly distinguishable major lines of business or geographical areas of operations that either have been disposed of or are classified as held for sale. IFRS 5 does not contain separate guidance on measuring discontinued operations. Profit or loss from discontinued operations is presented separately in the statement of comprehensive income.
Effective date:	Annual periods beginning on or after 1 January 2005. Earlier application is encouraged. Amendments resulting from IAS 1 (amended 2007) and IAS 27 (amended 2008) must be applied at the same time as the amended IAS 1 and IAS 27.
Applies to:	All entities

IFRS 5 Non-current Assets Held for Sale and Discontinued Operations (1/2)

Non-current assets held for sale

Definition

- The asset must be available for immediate sale and

- the sale must be highly probable, i.e. management must be committed to a plan to sell the asset, an active programme to locate a buyer must have been initiated, and the sale must generally be completed within 12 months. (6–11)

Measurement

- Measure the carrying amount in accordance with applicable IFRSs immediately before classification as held for sale
- Measure at the lower of carrying amount and fair value less costs to sell
- Discontinue depreciation/amortisation
- Recognise further write-downs to decreased fair value less costs to sell
- Recognise increases in value up to the amount of previously recognised impairment losses in accordance with IAS 36 or IFRS 5. (15–19)

Presentation/ Disclosure

- Present separately from other assets in the statement of financial position as a category of current assets (38)

- Present gains or losses on remeasurement in profit or loss from continuing operations unless the assets are components of a discontinued operation. (38)

Discontinued operations

Definition

A component of an entity that has either already been disposed of, or is classified as held for sale, and:
- that represents a separate major line of business or geographical area of operations and
- is part of a single coordinated plan to dispose of a separate major line of business or geographical area of operations, or
- is a subsidiary acquired exclusively with a view to resale. (32)

Measurement

There are no specific measurement requirements applicable to discontinued operations, i.e.:
- the non-current assets or disposal groups held for sale in the discontinued operation are measured in accordance with IFRS 5
- other assets are measured in accordance with applicable IFRSs.

Presentation/ Disclosure

- Separate disclosure of a single amount in the statement of comprehensive income comprising of the total of: (33, 33A)
  – the after-tax profit or loss from discontinued operations and
  – the after-tax gain or loss on measurement to fair value less costs to sell and on the disposal of assets
- Prior-period adjustments (34)
- Disclosures in the statement of comprehensive income items, the statement of cash flows and segment reporting. (33)

IFRS 5 Non-current Assets Held for Sale and Discontinued Operations (2/2)

Disposal groups held for sale

Definition

Disposal groups may include:
- non-current assets held for sale in accordance with IFRS 5;
- other assets and
- liabilities

to be disposed of together (App. A)

Measurement

- Measure the carrying amount of all assets and liabilities of the disposal group in accordance with applicable IFRSs immediately before classification as held for sale
- Measure at the lower of the carrying amount of the disposal group and the fair value less costs to sell of the disposal group
- Separate to the impairment test for the disposal group, assets and liabilities of the disposal group that do not fall within the scope of the measurement requirements of IFRS 5 are measured in accordance with applicable IFRSs. (15–19)

Presentation/ Disclosure

- Present the disposal group's liabilities separately in the statement of financial position; liabilities and assets may not be offset.
- Disclose the main categories of assets and liabilities in the notes; exemption for subsidiaries that were acquired exclusively with a view to resale (38–40)

KPMG

IFRS 6 Exploration for and Evaluation of Mineral Resources (amended 2006)

Scope:	Financial reporting for expenditures incurred for the exploration and evaluation of mineral resources
Scope exclusions:	Accounting for expenditures incurred before the entity has obtained the corresponding extraction rights, or after technical feasibility and commercial viability are demonstrable.
Core principles:	Expenditures incurred for the exploration and evaluation of mineral resources are measured at cost.
	The scope of such cost is not explicitly defined in IFRS 6. On the basis of an exemption from the application of IAS 8.11 and 12, an entity may therefore develop a specific accounting policy, ranging from immediate recognition as an expense through to recognition as an asset on the basis of direct and indirect costs.
	Depending on the nature of the assets recognised, they are classified as tangible and/or intangible assets. The standard models for subsequent measurement contained in IAS 16 and IAS 38 may then be applied in line with the classification of the assets.
	Special indications are applied for impairment testing, and assets are tested for impairment at a level not larger than the entity's segments.
Effective date:	Annual periods beginning on or after 1 January 2006. Earlier application is encouraged.
Applies to:	All entities

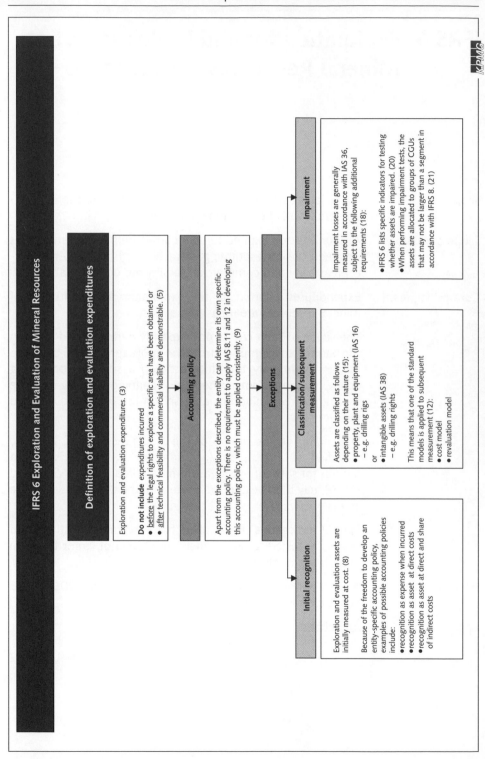

IFRS 6 Exploration and Evaluation of Mineral Resources

Definition of exploration and evaluation expenditures

Exploration and evaluation expenditures. (3)

Do not include expenditures incurred
• before the legal rights to explore a specific area have been obtained or
• after technical feasibility and commercial viability are demonstrable. (5)

Accounting policy

Apart from the exceptions described, the entity can determine its own specific accounting policy. There is no requirement to apply IAS 8.11 and 12 in developing this accounting policy, which must be applied consistently. (9)

Exceptions

Initial recognition

Exploration and evaluation assets are initially measured at cost. (8)

Because of the freedom to develop an entity-specific accounting policy, examples of possible accounting policies include:
• recognition as expense when incurred
• recognition as asset at direct costs
• recognition as asset at direct and share of indirect costs

Classification/subsequent measurement

Assets are classified as follows depending on their nature (15):
• property, plant and equipment (IAS 16)
 – e.g. drilling rigs
or
• intangible assets (IAS 38)
 – e.g. drilling rights

This means that one of the standard models is applied to subsequent measurement (12):
• cost model
• revaluation model

Impairment

Impairment losses are generally measured in accordance with IAS 36, subject to the following additional requirements (18):
• IFRS 6 lists specific indicators for testing whether assets are impaired. (20)
• When performing impairment tests, the assets are allocated to groups of CGUs that may not be larger than a segment in accordance with IFRS 8. (21)

IFRS 7 Financial Instruments: Disclosures
(amended 2008)

Scope:	Disclosures on financial instruments
Scope exclusions:	Recognition and measurement of financial instruments are governed by IAS 39, while IAS 32 addresses the presentation of financial instruments.
Core principles:	IFRS 7 classifies the required disclosures on financial instruments into those that relate directly to the financial statements and those that are more concerned with the entity's risk management.
	The disclosures related to the financial statements include disclosures about the effect of financial instruments on the statement of financial position and statement of comprehensive income and a description of the applicable accounting policies. They also include comprehensive disclosures on hedge accounting and fair values. Disclosures are also required for special cases, such as defaults and breaches, or transfers of financial assets that do not quality for derecognition.
	The risk-related disclosures comprise qualitative descriptions of the entity's risk management policies, classified into credit, liquidity and market risk. IFRS 7 also requires comprehensive quantitative disclosures on these risk categories. The quantitative disclosures should correspond to the information provided internally to the entity's key management personnel and include sensitivity analysis.
Effective date:	Annual periods beginning on or after 1 January 2007. Earlier application is encouraged. Amendments resulting from IAS 1 (amended 2007) and IFRS 3 (amended 2008) must be applied at the same time as the amended IAS 1 and IFRS 3.
Applies to:	All entities

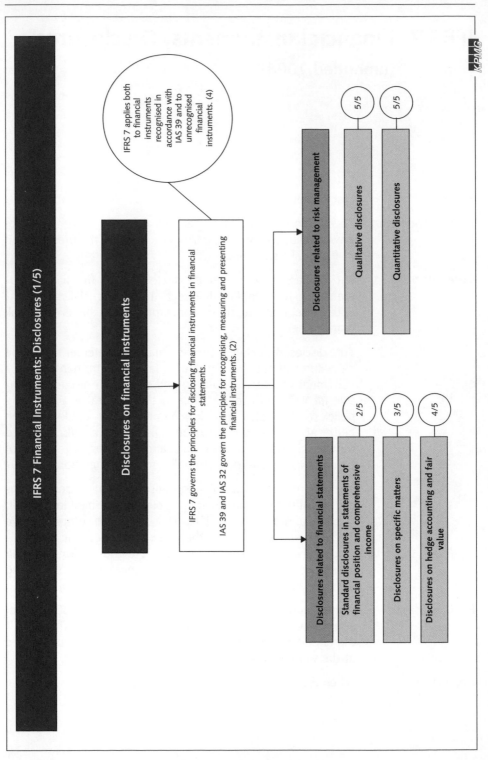

IFRS 7 Financial Instruments: Disclosures (1/5)

IFRS 7 applies both to financial instruments recognised in accordance with IAS 39 and to unrecognised financial instruments. (4)

Disclosures on financial instruments

IFRS 7 governs the principles for disclosing financial instruments in financial statements.

IAS 39 and IAS 32 govern the principles for recognising, measuring and presenting financial instruments. (2)

Disclosures related to risk management

Qualitative disclosures   5/5

Quantitative disclosures   5/5

Disclosures related to financial statements

Standard disclosures in statements of financial position and comprehensive income   2/5

Disclosures on specific matters   3/5

Disclosures on hedge accounting and fair value   4/5

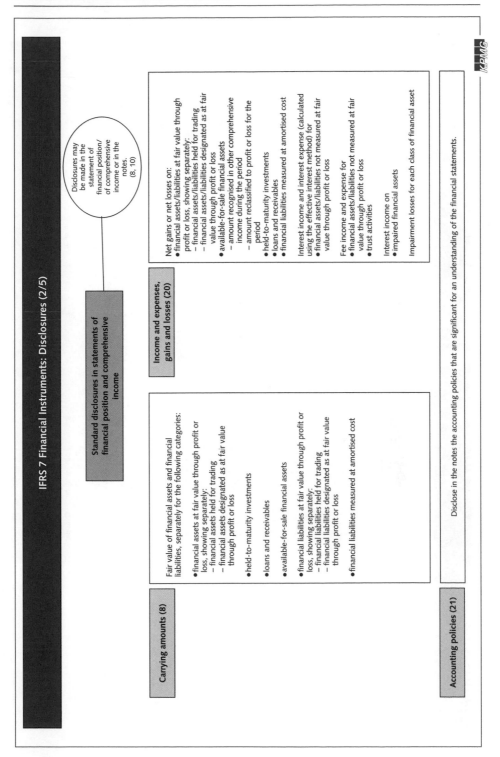

IFRS 7 Financial Instruments: Disclosures (2/5)

Standard disclosures in statements of financial position and comprehensive income

Disclosures may be made in the statement of financial position/ of comprehensive income or in the notes.
(8, 10)

Carrying amounts (8)

Fair value of financial assets and financial liabilities, separately for the following categories:

- financial assets at fair value through profit or loss, showing separately:
  - financial assets held for trading
  - financial assets designated as at fair value through profit or loss
- held-to-maturity investments
- loans and receivables
- available-for-sale financial assets

- financial liabilities at fair value through profit or loss, showing separately:
  - financial liabilities held for trading
  - financial liabilities designated as at fair value through profit or loss
- financial liabilities measured at amortised cost

Income and expenses, gains and losses (20)

Net gains or net losses on:
- financial assets/liabilities at fair value through profit or loss, showing separately:
  - financial assets/liabilities held for trading
  - financial assets/liabilities designated as at fair value through profit or loss
- available-for-sale financial assets
  - amount recognised in other comprehensive income during the period
  - amount reclassified to profit or loss for the period
- held-to-maturity investments
- loans and receivables
- financial liabilities measured at amortised cost

Interest income and interest expense (calculated using the effective interest method) for
- financial assets/liabilities not measured at fair value through profit or loss

Fee income and expense for
- financial assets/liabilities not measured at fair value through profit or loss
- trust activities

Interest income on
- impaired financial assets

Impairment losses for each class of financial asset

Accounting policies (21)

Disclose in the notes the accounting policies that are significant for an understanding of the financial statements.

IFRS 7 Financial Instruments: Disclosures (3/5)

Disclosures on specific matters

Credit risk (9–11)

For loans and receivables designated as at fair value through profit or loss:
- maximum exposure to credit risk
- mitigation of credit risk through credit derivatives and similar instruments
- change in fair value due to change in credit risk, for the period and cumulatively
- method for calculating those amounts

For financial liabilities designated as at fair value through profit or loss:
- change in fair value due to change in the credit risk of the liabilities, for the period and cumulatively
- method for calculating those amounts

Reclassification (12)

Reclassification from fair value measurement to measurement at amortised cost, or vice versa:
- amount
- reason for reclassification

Derecognition (13)

Disclosures on financial assets transferred but not derecognised:
- nature of the assets
- nature of remaining risks and rewards
- carrying amounts of the assets and associated liabilities; in the event of continuing involvement, the carrying amount of the original asset and the amount the entity continues to recognise

Collateral (14–15)

Financial assets pledged as collateral:
- carrying amount of the assets
- terms and conditions of the pledge

Collateral held:
- fair value of collateral held
- fair value of collateral sold
- terms and conditions of use of the collateral

Allowance account for credit losses (16)

Disclose changes in allowance accounts during the period for each class of financial assets

Compound financial instruments (17)

Financial instrument with multiple embedded derivatives whose values are interdependent:
- disclose the features

Defaults and breaches (18–19)

Disclose for defaults of loans payable during the period:
- Details of defaults
  - principal
  - interest
  - sinking fund
  - redemption terms
- carrying amount
- any remedy or renegotiation before financial statements were authorised for issue

KPMG

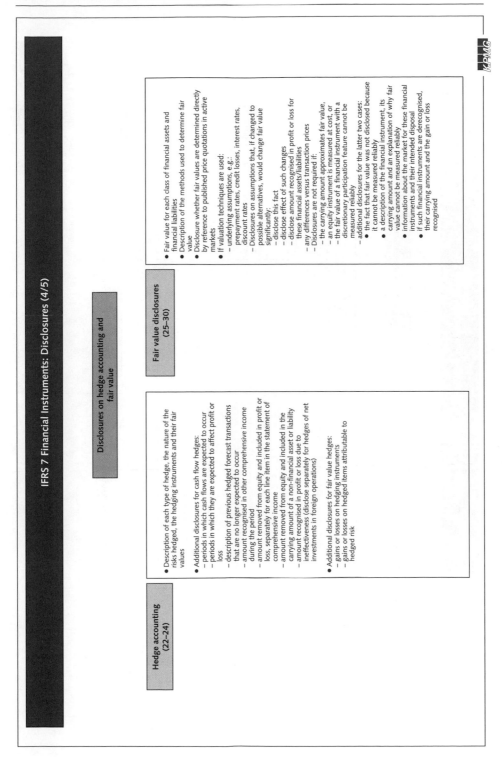

IFRS 7 Financial Instruments: Disclosures (4/5)

Disclosures on hedge accounting and fair value

Hedge accounting (22–24)

- Description of each type of hedge, the nature of the risks hedged, the hedging instruments and their fair values
- Additional disclosures for cash flow hedges:
  - periods in which cash flows are expected to occur
  - periods in which they are expected to affect profit or loss
  - description of previous hedged forecast transactions that are no longer expected to occur
  - amount recognised in other comprehensive income during the period
  - amount removed from equity and included in profit or loss, separately for each line item in the statement of comprehensive income
  - amount removed from equity and included in the carrying amount of a non-financial asset or liability
  - amount recognised in profit or loss due to ineffectiveness (disclose separately for hedges of net investments in foreign operations)
- Additional disclosures for fair value hedges:
  - gains or losses on hedging instruments
  - gains or losses on hedged items attributable to hedged risk

Fair value disclosures (25–30)

- Fair value for each class of financial assets and financial liabilities
- Description of the methods used to determine fair value
- Disclosure whether fair values are determined directly by reference to published price quotations in active markets
- If valuation techniques are used:
  - underlying assumptions, e.g.: prepayment rates, credit losses, interest rates, discount rates
  - Disclosures on assumptions that, if changed to possible alternatives, would change fair value significantly:
    - disclose this fact
    - disclose effect of such changes
    - disclose amount recognised in profit or loss for these financial assets/liabilities
  - any differences versus transaction prices
  - Disclosures are not required if:
    - the carrying amount approximates fair value,
    - an equity instrument is measured at cost, or
    - the fair value of a financial instrument with a discretionary participation feature cannot be measured reliably
    - additional disclosures for the latter two cases:
      - the fact that fair value was not disclosed because it cannot be measured reliably
      - a description of the financial instrument, its carrying amount and an explanation of why fair value cannot be measured reliably
      - information about the market for these financial instruments and their intended disposal
      - if such financial instruments are derecognised, their carrying amount and the gain or loss recognised

IFRS 7 Financial Instruments: Disclosures (5/5)

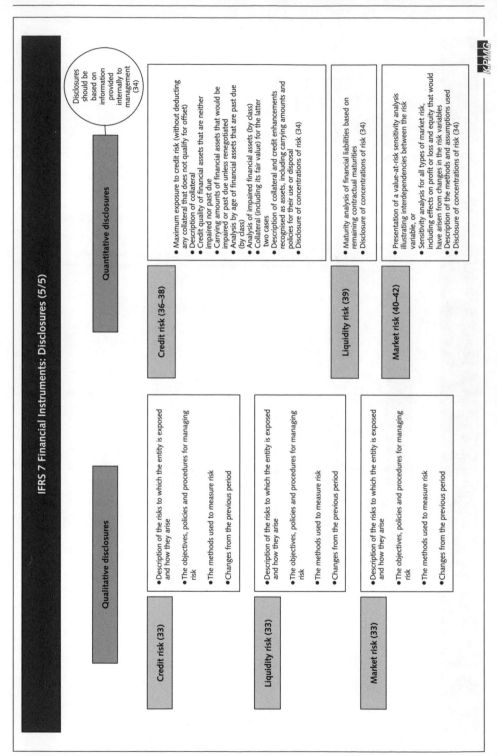

Disclosures should be based on information provided internally to management (34)

Qualitative disclosures

Credit risk (33)
- Description of the risks to which the entity is exposed and how they arise
- The objectives, policies and procedures for managing risk
- The methods used to measure risk
- Changes from the previous period

Liquidity risk (33)
- Description of the risks to which the entity is exposed and how they arise
- The objectives, policies and procedures for managing risk
- The methods used to measure risk
- Changes from the previous period

Market risk (33)
- Description of the risks to which the entity is exposed and how they arise
- The objectives, policies and procedures for managing risk
- The methods used to measure risk
- Changes from the previous period

Quantitative disclosures

Credit risk (36–38)
- Maximum exposure to credit risk (without deducting any collateral that does not qualify for offset)
- Description of collateral
- Credit quality of financial assets that are neither impaired nor past due
- Carrying amounts of financial assets that would be impaired or past due unless renegotiated
- Analysis by age of financial assets that are past due (by class)
- Analysis of impaired financial assets (by class)
- Collateral (including its fair value) for the latter two cases
- Description of collateral and credit enhancements recognised as assets, including carrying amounts and policies for their use or disposal
- Disclosure of concentrations of risk (34)

Liquidity risk (39)
- Maturity analysis of financial liabilities based on remaining contractual maturities
- Disclosure of concentrations of risk (34)

Market risk (40–42)
- Presentation of a value-at-risk sensitivity analysis illustrating interdependencies between the risk variable, or
- Sensitivity analysis for all types of market risk, including effects on profit or loss and equity that would have arisen from changes in the risk variables
- Description of the methods and assumptions used
- Disclosure of concentrations of risk (34)

KPMG

IFRS 8 Operating Segments (amended 2008)

Scope:	Segment reporting
Scope exclusions:	–
Core principles:	Reportable segments are based on internally reported operating segments (management approach). If the revenue, profit or loss, or assets of an operating segment amount to at least 10% of the combined amounts of all the entity's operating segments, the operating segment is a reportable segment.
	A measure of profit or loss and total assets must be disclosed for each reportable segment. Specified other amounts from the statement of comprehensive income and the statement of financial position must be disclosed but only if they are included in the measure of segment profit or loss or the measure of total assets, or are otherwise regularly provided to the chief operating decision maker for review. All amounts disclosed must comply with the internally reported measurement methods. Reconciliations of certain items to the financial statements and explanations of the measurement methods used are required.
	The following entity-wide disclosures must also be made: revenues from external customers classified by individual product/service or group of products/services; revenues from external customers and certain non-current assets classified by the entity's country of domicile and foreign countries; and, in the case of revenues from major customers, an entity must disclose the amounts and the segments in which the revenues are reported. Entity-wide disclosures must correspond to the amounts in the financial statements.
Effective date:	Annual periods beginning on or after 1 January 2009. Earlier application is permitted. IAS 14 must be applied until this date.
Applies to:	Only publicly traded entities

IFRS 8 Operating Segments (1/4)

(2/4) **Simplified overview**

Segment disclosures

	Reportable segments A B C D	Other segments & activities

Revenues from external customers
Intersegment revenues
Interest revenue
Interest expense
Depreciation and amortisation
Material items of income and expense
Interest in profit or loss of equity-accounted investments
Income tax expense or income
Other material non-cash items
Assets
Carrying amount of equity-accounted investments
Additions to non-current assets
Liabilities

Reconciliations of the total of the reportable segments to the amount in the financial statements of:
- Revenues
- Profit or loss
- Assets
- Liabilities
- Other material items

Explanations of the **differences** between the accounting policies applied and the accounting policies used in the financial statements

(3/4)

Entity-wide disclosures

(4/4)

Revenues by product/service

Product/service (group) I

Product/service (group) II

Product/service (group) III

Revenues as reported in the financial statements

Revenues and assets by geographical area

	Country of dom.	Foreign countries	Amount in financial statements
Revenues			
Non-current assets			

Revenues by major customer

	Revenues included in segment(s):
Revenues from major customer 1	
Revenues from major customer 2	
Revenues from major customer 3	

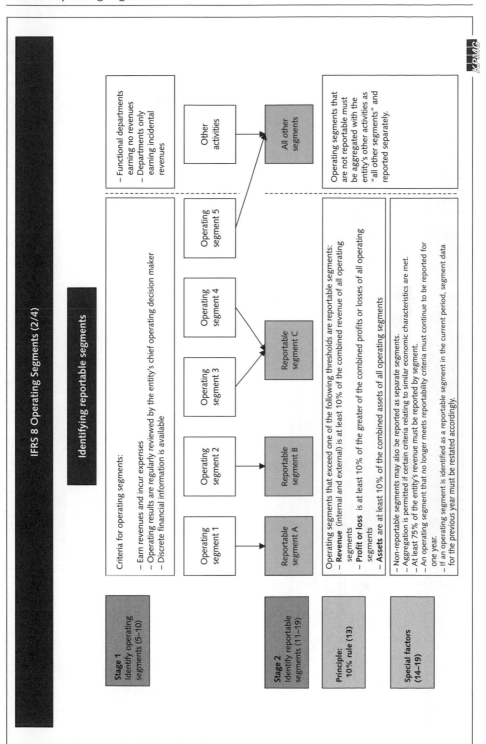

IFRS 8 Operating Segments (2/4)

Identifying reportable segments

Stage 1
Identify operating segments (5–10)

Criteria for operating segments:

– Earn revenues and incur expenses
– Operating results are regularly reviewed by the entity's chief operating decision maker
– Discrete financial information is available

| Operating segment 1 | Operating segment 2 | Operating segment 3 | Operating segment 4 | Operating segment 5 | Other activities |

– Functional departments earning no revenues
– Departments only earning incidental revenues

| Reportable segment A | Reportable segment B | Reportable segment C | All other segments |

Stage 2
Identify reportable segments (11–19)

Principle:
10% rule (13)

Operating segments that exceed one of the following thresholds are reportable segments:
– **Revenue** (internal and external) is at least 10% of the combined revenue of all operating segments
– **Profit or loss** is at least 10% of the greater of the combined profits or losses of all operating segments
– **Assets** are at least 10% of the combined assets of all operating segments

Special factors
(14–19)

– Non-reportable segments may also be reported as separate segments.
– Aggregation is permitted if certain criteria relating to similar economic characteristics are met.
– At least 75% of the entity's revenue must be reported by segment.
– An operating segment that no longer meets reportability criteria must continue to be reported for one year.
– If an operating segment is identified as a reportable segment in the current period, segment data for the previous year must be restated accordingly.

Operating segments that are not reportable must be aggregated with the entity's other activities as "all other segments" and reported separately.

IFRS 8 Operating Segments (3/4)

Segment disclosures

Amounts in acc. with internal measurement methods (25,26)

Segment disclosures

Statement of comprehensive income (23)

1) Measure of profit or loss

2) —

3) Revenues from external customers

Intersegment revenues

Interest revenue

Interest expense 4)

Depreciation and amortisation

Material items of income and expense

Interest in profit or loss of equity-accounted investments

Income tax expense or income

Other material non-cash items (other than depreciation and amortisation)

Statement of financial position (23, 24)

Measure of total assets

Measure of liabilities

Carrying amount of equity-accounted investments

Additions to non-current assets (other than financial instruments, deferred tax assets, post-employment benefit assets, rights under insurance contracts)

Explanations

Reconciliations (28, 21)

- All material reconciling items must be separately identified and described
- Reported for each period presented
- Reconciliations are required in each case from the total of all reportable segments to the figures in the financial statements for... :

Revenues

Profit or loss before tax expense and discontinued operations

Assets

Liabilities

Other material items

Measurement methods (27)

Explanations of the measurement methods applied to... :

Transactions between reportable segments

Differences in the measurement methods compared with the financial statements for:
- Profit or loss
- Assets
- Liabilities

Changes in measurement methods used to determine profit or loss (including effects)

Nature and effect of any asymmetrical allocations

---

1) Must always be disclosed.

2) Disclosed if regularly provided to the chief operating decision maker.

3) Disclosed if contained in the measure of profit or loss/total assets that is regularly reviewed by the chief operating decision maker or regularly provided to the chief operating decision maker, even if the amount is not included in the measure of profit or loss/total assets.

4) Interest expense and revenue may be reported net if interest revenue accounts for the majority of the segments revenue and the chief operating decision maker uses the net amount to make decisions.

KPMG

IFRS 8 Operating Segments (4/4)

Entity-wide disclosures

Amounts in acc. with measurement methods used for financial statements (31–34)

Revenues by product/service (32)

Revenues from external customers must be broken down into:

Individual products and services or groups of similar products and services.

Amounts are not disclosed if they are not available and the cost to develop the information would be excessive. This fact must be disclosed.

Revenues and assets by geographical area (33)

Revenues from external customers must be classified into:

• Revenues from customers in the entity's country of domicile and
• Revenues from customers in foreign countries.

Material foreign countries must be disclosed separately.

Amounts are not disclosed if they are not available and the cost to develop the information would be excessive. This fact must be disclosed.

Non-current assets
(other than financial instruments, deferred tax assets, post-employment benefit assets, rights under insurance contracts) must be classified into:

• Assets in the entity's country of domicile and
• Assets in foreign countries.

Material foreign countries must be disclosed separately.

Amounts are not disclosed if they are not available and the cost to develop the information would be excessive. This fact must be disclosed.

Information on revenues by major customer (34)

The following disclosures are required for **revenues** from individual customers that account for more than 10% of total revenues:

• revenues from each such customer and
• the segment(s) reporting the revenues.

Customers known to be under common control count as a single customer.

The names of the customers need not be disclosed.

KPMG

III. IFRIC Interpretations

IFRIC 1 Changes in Existing Decommissioning, Restoration and Similar Liabilities

References:	IAS 1, IAS 8, IAS 16, IAS 23, IAS 36, IAS 37
Core principles:	Provisions for decommissioning, restoration and similar liabilities that have been recognised in accordance with IAS 37 and have also been recognised as part of the cost of assets in accordance with IAS 16.16 c) may change over time because of changes in the estimated settlement date, the estimated cash flows required to settle the obligation, or the discount rate.
	In the case of an asset measured using the cost model, changes in the provision are added to or deducted from the carrying amount of the asset in the current period. If the amount of any deduction exceeds the carrying amount of the asset, the excess is recognised as income. An increase in the provision accompanied by an increase in the asset's carrying amount may be an indication of impairment.
	In the case of assets measured using the revaluation model, changes in the provision generally increase or decrease the revaluation surplus.
	In both cases, the adjusted depreciable amount of the asset is depreciated over the remaining useful life.
	In contrast, changes due to the unwinding of the discount are recognised as interest expense.
Effective date:	Annual periods beginning on or after 1 September 2004. Earlier application is encouraged.

IFRIC 1 Changes in Existing Decommissioning, Restoration and Similar Liabilities

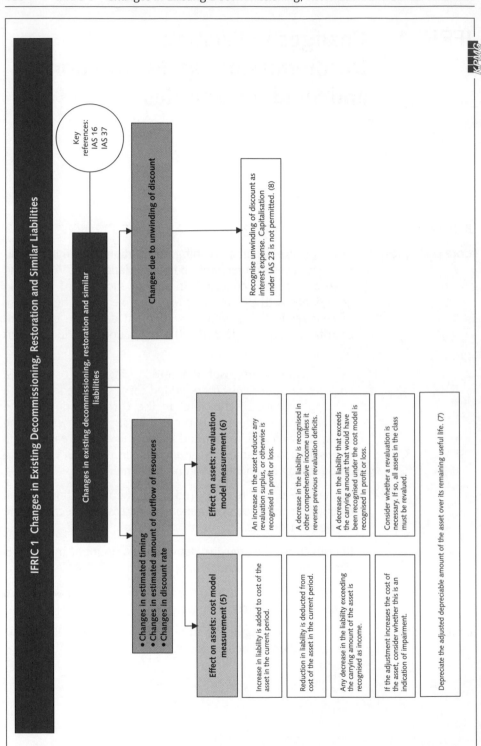

Key references:
IAS 16
IAS 37

Changes in existing decommissioning, restoration and similar liabilities

- Changes in estimated timing
- Changes in estimated amount of outflow of resources
- Changes in discount rate

Changes due to unwinding of discount

Recognise unwinding of discount as interest expense. Capitalisation under IAS 23 is not permitted. (8)

Effect on assets: cost model measurement (5)

Increase in liability is added to cost of the asset in the current period.

Reduction in liability is deducted from cost of the asset in the current period.

Any decrease in the liability exceeding the carrying amount of the asset is recognised as income.

If the adjustment increases the cost of the asset, consider whether this is an indication of impairment.

Depreciate the adjusted depreciable amount of the asset over its remaining useful life. (7)

Effect on assets: revaluation model measurement (6)

An increase in the asset reduces any revaluation surplus, or otherwise is recognised in profit or loss.

A decrease in the liability is recognised in other comprehensive income unless it reverses previous revaluation deficits.

A decrease in the liability that exceeds the carrying amount that would have been recognised under the cost model is recognised in profit or loss.

Consider whether a revaluation is necessary. If so, all assets in the class must be revalued.

IFRIC 2   Members' Shares in Co-Operative Entities and Similar Instruments

References:	IAS 32, IAS 39
Core principles:	If the holder of a member's share is entitled to request redemption for cash or another financial asset ('puttable instrument'), IAS 32.18 b requires this member's share to be recognised by the entity as a financial liability, rather than equity.
	IFRIC 2 states that a puttable instrument is classified as a financial liability if the entity does not have an unconditional right to refuse redemption. The probability of an outflow of resources is therefore not a decisive factor.
	If the entity only has to right to refuse redemption under certain conditions, e.g. if certain liquidity criteria are met or not met, the member's share is a puttable instrument because the entity does not have an unconditional right to refuse redemption.
	If there is an unconditional right to refuse redemption for some of the members' shares, those shares are classified as equity.
	If a member's share is classified as a financial liability, interest, dividends and other returns on that share are recognised as expenses.
	The principles described above apply to all legal forms, not only to co-operatives.
Effective date:	Annual periods beginning on or after 1 January 2005. Earlier application is allowed.

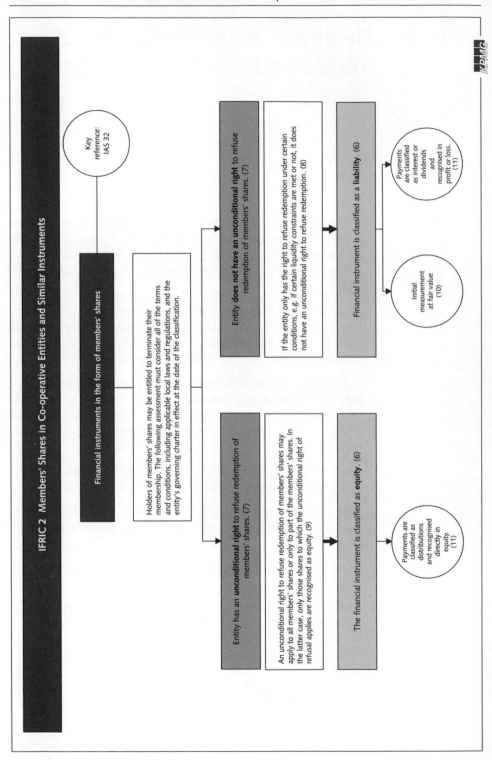

IFRIC 2   Members' Shares in Co-operative Entities and Similar Instruments

Key reference: IAS 32

Financial instruments in the form of members' shares

Holders of members' shares may be entitled to terminate their membership. The following assessment must consider all of the terms and conditions, including applicable local laws and regulations, and the entity's governing charter in effect at the date of the classification.

Entity has an **unconditional right** to refuse redemption of members' shares. (7)

An unconditional right to refuse redemption of members' shares may apply to all members' shares or only to part of the members' shares. In the latter case, only those shares to which the unconditional right of refusal applies are recognised as equity. (9)

The financial instrument is classified as **equity**. (6)

Payments are classified as distributions and recognised directly in equity. (11)

Entity **does not have an unconditional right** to refuse redemption of members' shares. (7)

If the entity only has the right to refuse redemption under certain conditions, e.g. if certain liquidity constraints are met or not, it does not have an unconditional right to refuse redemption. (8)

Financial instrument is classified as a **liability**. (6)

Initial measurement at fair value (10)

Payments are classified as interest or dividends and recognised in profit or loss. (11)

IFRIC 4 Determining whether an Arrangement contains a Lease

References:	IAS 8, IAS 16, IAS 17, IAS 38
Core principles:	A lease generally describes an arrangement under which an asset is used in return for payment. In accordance with IAS 17, leases are classified as operating leases or finance leases.
	IFRIC 4 states that an arrangement also contains a lease if fulfilment of the arrangement (e.g. delivery of goods) depends on the use of a specific asset (or group of assets) and the recipient (indirectly) receives the right to use the asset.
	Fulfilment of the arrangement depends on the use of a specific asset if the asset that will be used for delivery is explicitly identified in the arrangement, or if the supplier owns only one asset to fulfil the obligation and it is not economically feasible or practicable for the supplier to perform its obligation through the use of alternative assets.
	The right to use the asset is conveyed to the recipient if the recipient can control the use of the asset, for example by operating it or controlling physical access to it.
	If both of these conditions are met (which must be assessed at the inception of the arrangement), the lease must be classified as an operating lease or a finance lease in accordance with IAS 17.
Effective date:	Annual periods beginning on or after 1 January 2006. Earlier application is encouraged.

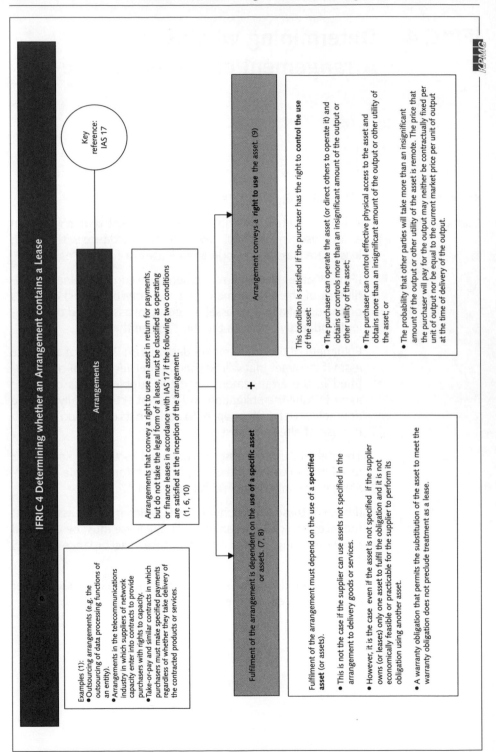

IFRIC 4 Determining whether an Arrangement contains a Lease

Key reference: IAS 17

Arrangements

Arrangements that convey a right to use an asset in return for payments, but do not take the legal form of a lease, must be classified as operating or finance leases in accordance with IAS 17 if the following two conditions are satisfied at the inception of the arrangement: (1, 6, 10)

Examples (1):
- Outsourcing arrangements (e.g. the outsourcing of data processing functions of an entity).
- Arrangements in the telecommunications industry in which suppliers of network capacity enter into contracts to provide purchasers with rights to capacity.
- Take-or-pay and similar contracts in which purchasers must make specified payments regardless of whether they take delivery of the contracted products or services.

Fulfilment of the arrangement is dependent on the use of a specific asset or assets. (7, 8)

Fulfilment of the arrangement must depend on the use of a **specified asset** (or assets).
- This is not the case if the supplier can use assets not specified in the arrangement to delivery goods or services.
- However, it is the case even if the asset is not specified if the supplier owns (or leases) only one asset to fulfil the obligation and it is not economically feasible or practicable for the supplier to perform its obligation using another asset.
- A warranty obligation that permits the substitution of the asset to meet the warranty obligation does not preclude treatment as a lease.

+

Arrangement conveys a right to use the asset. (9)

This condition is satisfied if the purchaser has the right to **control the use** of the asset:
- The purchaser can operate the asset (or direct others to operate it) and obtains or controls more than an insignificant amount of the output or other utility of the asset;
- The purchaser can control effective physical access to the asset and obtains more than an insignificant amount of the output or other utility of the asset; or
- The probability that other parties will take more than an insignificant amount of the output or other utility of the asset is remote. The price that the purchaser will pay for the output may neither be contractually fixed per unit of output nor be equal to the current market price per unit of output at the time of delivery of the output.

IFRIC 5 Rights to Interests arising from Decommissioning, Restoration and Environmental Rehabilitation Funds

References:	IAS 8, IAS 27, IAS 28, IAS 31, IAS 37, IAS 39
Core principles:	Entities with significant decommissioning, restoration and environmental rehabilitation obligations often segregate assets into separate funds. The funds use the assets to invest and to reimburse the entity or entities that contribute to the funds for the decommissioning costs they incur subsequently.
	IFRIC 5 describes the accounting treatment for interests in funds whose assets are administered separately and to which the entity/entities has/have restricted access.
	The entity accounts for the decommissioning obligations themselves as provisions in accordance with IAS 37.
	The reimbursement rights are accounted for as subsidiaries, joint ventures, or associates, depending on the extent of the entity's control or influence over the fund. If the entity's influence is less than significant, the reimbursement right is accounted for in accordance with IAS 37 at the lower of the carrying amount of the provision and the fair value of the reimbursement right.
	Any residual interest of the entity in the fund that extends beyond the mere right to reimbursement is accounted for as a financial instrument in accordance with IAS 39.
Effective date:	Annual periods beginning on or after 1 January 2006. Earlier application is encouraged.

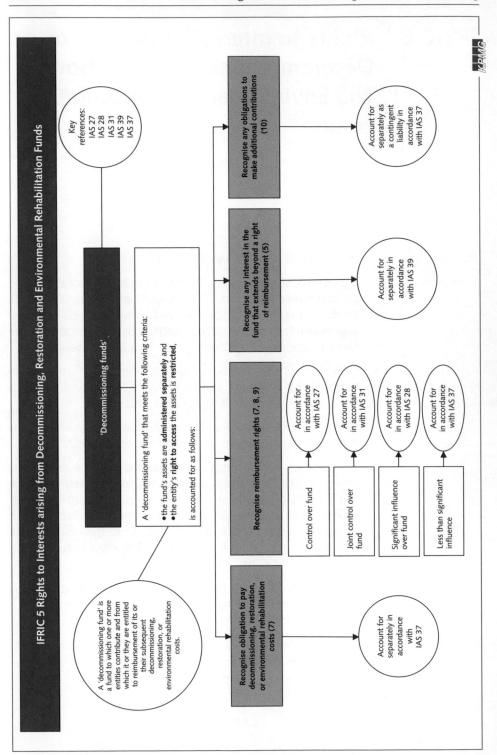

IFRIC 5 Rights to Interests arising from Decommissioning, Restoration and Environmental Rehabilitation Funds

Key references:
IAS 27
IAS 28
IAS 31
IAS 39
IAS 37

A 'decommissioning fund' is a fund to which one or more entities contribute and from which it or they are entitled to reimbursement of its or their subsequent decommissioning, restoration, or environmental rehabilitation costs.

'Decommissioning funds'

A 'decommissioning fund' that meets the following criteria:
• the fund's assets are administered separately and
• the entity's right to access the assets is restricted,

is accounted for as follows:

Recognise obligation to pay decommissioning, restoration, or environmental rehabilitation costs (7)

Account for separately in accordance with IAS 37

Recognise reimbursement rights (7, 8, 9)

Control over fund → Account for in accordance with IAS 27

Joint control over fund → Account for in accordance with IAS 31

Significant influence over fund → Account for in accordance with IAS 28

Less than significant influence → Account for in accordance with IAS 37

Recognise any interest in the fund that extends beyond a right of reimbursement (5)

Account for separately in accordance with IAS 39

Recognise any obligations to make additional contributions (10)

Account for separately as a contingent liability in accordance with IAS 37

IFRIC 6 Liabilities arising from Participating in a Specific Market – Waste Electrical and Electronic Equipment

References:	IAS 8, IAS 37
Core principles:	The EU Directive on Waste Electrical and Electronic Equipment governs responsibility for the collection and recycling or disposal of waste electrical and electronic equipment. It distinguishes between 'historical' waste – which is waste relating to products sold before 13 August 2005 – and 'new' waste. The directive also distinguishes between waste from private households and waste from sources other than private households (i.e. commercial waste).
	IFRIC 6 states that producers of historical waste household equipment must recognise provisions for waste management costs because of their liability under EU law. However, neither the manufacture nor the sale of the equipment is the obligating event for the recognition of a provision. Rather, the producer's participation in the market during the measurement period constitutes the obligating event.
	Although IFRIC 6 does not directly specify that provisions must be recognised for new waste from private households, the principle described above can also be applied, provided that national rules governing new waste are similar to those governing historical waste.
	IFRIC 6 does not address commercial waste, and the general principles for recognising provisions in accordance with IAS 37 apply to commercial waste.
	Equally, IFRIC 6 does not address measurement issues.
Effective date:	Annual periods beginning on or after 1 December 2005. Earlier application is encouraged.

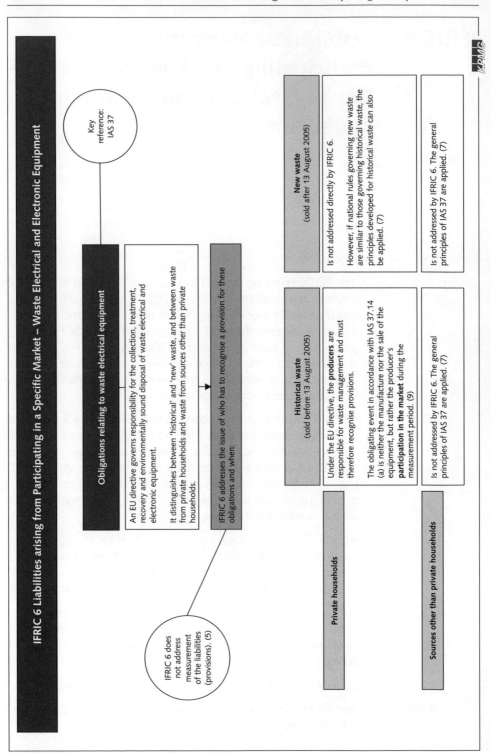

IFRIC 6 Liabilities arising from Participating in a Specific Market – Waste Electrical and Electronic Equipment

Key reference: IAS 37

Obligations relating to waste electrical equipment

An EU directive governs responsibility for the collection, treatment, recovery and environmentally sound disposal of waste electrical and electronic equipment.

It distinguishes between 'historical' and 'new' waste, and between waste from private households and waste from sources other than private households.

IFRIC 6 addresses the issue of who has to recognise a provision for these obligations and when:

IFRIC 6 does not address measurement of the liabilities (provisions). (5)

Private households

Historical waste
(sold before 13 August 2005)

Under the EU directive, the **producers** are responsible for waste management and must therefore recognise provisions.

The obligating event in accordance with IAS 37.14 (a) is neither the manufacture nor the sale of the equipment, but rather the producer's **participation in the market** during the measurement period. (9)

Is not addressed by IFRIC 6. The general principles of IAS 37 are applied. (7)

New waste
(sold after 13 August 2005)

Is not addressed directly by IFRIC 6.

However, if national rules governing new waste are similar to those governing historical waste, the principles developed for historical waste can also be applied. (7)

Is not addressed by IFRIC 6. The general principles of IAS 37 are applied. (7)

Sources other than private households

IFRIC 7 Applying the Restatement Approach under IAS 29

References:	IAS 12, IAS 29
Core principles:	In accordance with IAS 29, financial statements prepared in the currency of a hyperinflationary economy must be presented in the measuring unit current at the end of the reporting period.

IFRIC 7 explains the restatement methodology used for the first reporting period in which hyperinflation as defined by IAS 29 is identified, and for subsequent periods.

In the first period, the carrying amounts of non-monetary assets measured at historical cost in the opening statement of financial position for the earliest period presented in the financial statements are restated to reflect the effect of inflation from the date the assets were acquired or produced until the end of the reporting period.

Other non-monetary assets at the beginning of the earliest period presented in the financial statements are restated to reflect the effect of inflation from the date of the most recent revaluation until the end of the reporting period.

In the first step, deferred taxes in the opening statement of financial position for the reporting period are recognised and measured for the restated carrying amounts. They are then restated to reflect the effect of inflation during the reporting period.

In subsequent periods, the items are restated to reflect changes in the measuring unit for the subsequent period, although the change is only applied to the previous reporting period.

Effective date:	Annual periods beginning on or after 1 March 2006. Earlier application is encouraged.

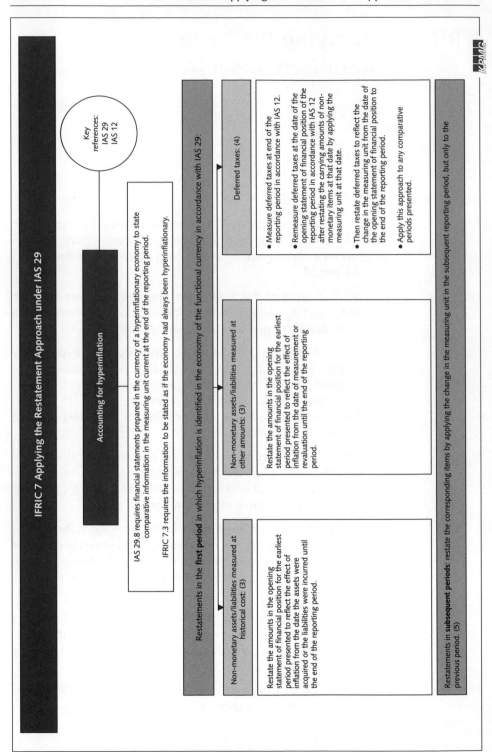

IFRIC 7 Applying the Restatement Approach under IAS 29

Key references:
IAS 29
IAS 12

Accounting for hyperinflation

IAS 29.8 requires financial statements prepared in the currency of a hyperinflationary economy to state comparative information in the measuring unit current at the end of the reporting period.

IFRIC 7.3 requires the information to be stated as if the economy had always been hyperinflationary.

Restatements in the **first period** in which hyperinflation is identified in the economy of the functional currency in accordance with IAS 29:

Non-monetary assets/liabilities measured at historical cost: (3)

Restate the amounts in the opening statement of financial position for the earliest period presented to reflect the effect of inflation from the date the assets were acquired or the liabilities were incurred until the end of the reporting period.

Non-monetary assets/liabilities measured at other amounts: (3)

Restate the amounts in the opening statement of financial position for the earliest period presented to reflect the effect of inflation from the date of measurement or revaluation until the end of the reporting period.

Deferred taxes: (4)

- Measure deferred taxes at end of the reporting period in accordance with IAS 12.
- Remeasure deferred taxes at the date of the opening statement of financial position of the reporting period in accordance with IAS 12 after restating the carrying amounts of non-monetary items at that date by applying the measuring unit at that date.
- Then restate deferred taxes to reflect the change in the measuring unit from the date of the opening statement of financial position to the end of the reporting period.
- Apply this approach to any comparative periods presented.

Restatements in **subsequent periods**: restate the corresponding items by applying the change in the measuring unit in the subsequent reporting period, but only to the previous period. (5)

IFRIC 8   Scope of IFRS 2

References:	IFRS 2, IAS 8
Core principles:	IFRS 2 applies to share-based payment transactions in which equity instruments (e.g. shares or stock options) and/or a cash settlement are granted as consideration for goods and services received.
	There were doubts as to whether IFRS 2 also applies to share-based payment transactions in which the entity cannot identify specifically some or all of the goods or services received. For example, this may be the case if shares are granted to a charitable organisation without any specific consideration.
	IFRIC 8 clarifies that IFRS 2 also applies to such share-based payment transactions in which the entity cannot identify some or all of the consideration received.
	IFRIC 8 distinguishes between identifiable and unidentifiable goods and services:
	Identifiable goods and services are measured in accordance with IFRS 2.
	Unidentifiable goods and services are measured as the difference between the fair value of the share-based payment and the fair value of the identifiable goods and services.
	As a rule, the goods and services are measured at the grant date. For cash-settled transactions, the liability must be remeasured at the end of each reporting period.
Effective date:	Annual periods beginning on or after 1 May 2006. Earlier application is encouraged.

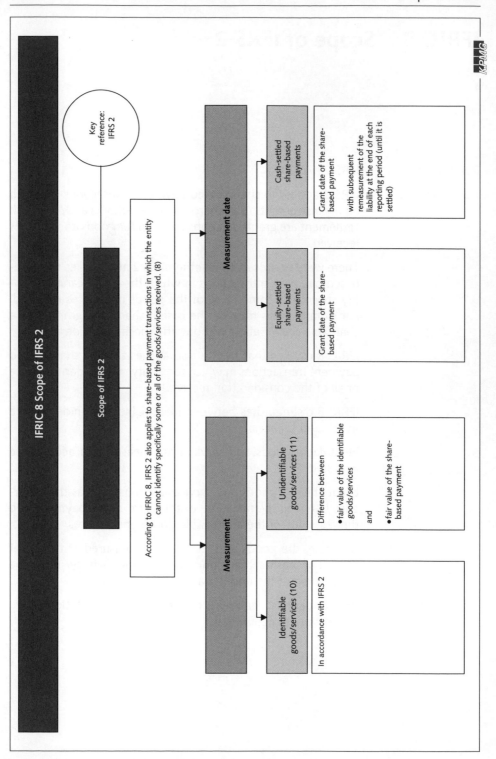

IFRIC 9 Reassessment of Embedded Derivatives

References:	IFRS 1, IAS 39
Core principles:	Under IAS 39.11, an entity must use certain criteria to assess whether an embedded derivative will be separated from a host contract and accounted for as a derivative in its own right in accordance with IAS 39. The Standard does not specify the timing of the assessment.
	IFRIC 9 clarifies that such assessment may only be made when the entity first becomes a party to the contract. Subsequent reassessment is therefore generally prohibited. However, reassessment is required if, at a later date, there is a substantial change in the terms of the contract that significantly modifies the expected cash flows under the contract.
	IFRIC 9 also clarifies that first-time adopters should not make their assessment on the basis of the conditions prevailing when they adopted IFRSs for the first time. Rather, they should use as a basis the conditions that existed at the earlier of the date at which they first became a party to the contract and the date a subsequent reassessment would have been required under IFRIC 9.
Effective date:	Annual periods beginning on or after 1 June 2006. Earlier application is encouraged.

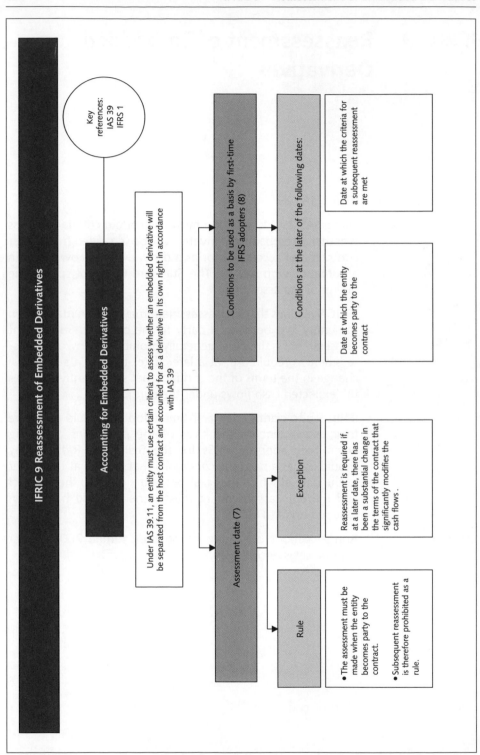

IFRIC 9 Reassessment of Embedded Derivatives

Key references:
IAS 39
IFRS 1

Accounting for Embedded Derivatives

Under IAS 39.11, an entity must use certain criteria to assess whether an embedded derivative will be separated from the host contract and accounted for as a derivative in its own right in accordance with IAS 39

Conditions to be used as a basis by first-time IFRS adopters (8)

Conditions at the later of the following dates:

Date at which the entity becomes party to the contract

Date at which the criteria for a subsequent reassessment are met

Assessment date (7)

Exception

Reassessment is required if, at a later date, there has been a substantial change in the terms of the contract that significantly modifies the cash flows .

Rule

• The assessment must be made when the entity becomes party to the contract.

• Subsequent reassessment is therefore prohibited as a rule.

IFRIC 10 Interim Financial Reporting and Impairment

References:	IAS 34, IAS 36, IAS 39
Core principles:	Impairment losses on goodwill, on financial assets carried at cost and on equity instruments classified as available for sale may not be reversed in subsequent periods or, in the latter case, may not be reversed through profit or loss (IAS 36.124, IAS 39.66, IAS 39.69).

This gives rise to the following conflict in IAS 34 *Interim Financial Reporting*:

On the one hand, IAS 34.28 sentence 1 requires that an entity apply the same accounting policies in its interim financial statements as are applied in its year-end financial statements. This means that previous impairment losses on the above-mentioned assets may not be reversed in interim financial statements.

On the other hand, under IAS 34.28 sentence 2, the frequency of an entity's reporting (annual, half-yearly, or quarterly) may not affect the measurement of its annual results. To achieve that objective, measurements for interim reporting purposes are made on a year-to-date basis. Impairment losses from previous interim financial statements must therefore be reversed in the current interim financial statements if the amount of the impairment loss has fallen in the meantime.

IFRIC 10 resolves this conflict by stating that impairment losses on the above-mentioned assets recognised in previous interim reporting periods may not be reversed.

IFRIC 10 contains an express statement that the consensus may not be extended by analogy to other areas of potential conflict between IAS 34 and other Standards.

Effective date:	Annual periods beginning on or after 1 November 2006. Earlier application is encouraged.

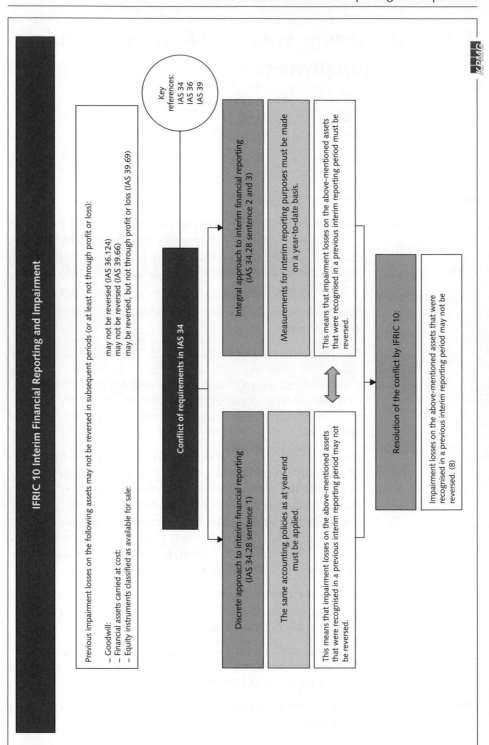

IFRIC 10 Interim Financial Reporting and Impairment

Previous impairment losses on the following assets may not be reversed in subsequent periods (or at least not through profit or loss):

- Goodwill: may not be reversed (IAS 36.124)
- Financial assets carried at cost: may not be reversed (IAS 39.66)
- Equity instruments classified as available for sale: may be reversed, but not through profit or loss (IAS 39.69)

Key references:
IAS 34
IAS 36
IAS 39

Conflict of requirements in IAS 34

Discrete approach to interim financial reporting (IAS 34.28 sentence 1)

The same accounting policies as at year-end must be applied.

This means that impairment losses on the above-mentioned assets that were recognised in a previous interim reporting period may not be reversed.

Integral approach to interim financial reporting (IAS 34.28 sentence 2 and 3)

Measurements for interim reporting purposes must be made on a year-to-date basis.

This means that impairment losses on the above-mentioned assets that were recognised in a previous interim reporting period must be reversed.

Resolution of the conflict by IFRIC 10:

Impairment losses on the above-mentioned assets that were recognised in a previous interim reporting period may not be reversed. (8)

IFRIC 11 IFRS 2 – Group and Treasury Share Transactions

References:	IAS 8, IAS 2, IAS 32
Core principles:	IFRS 2 governs accounting for share-based payment transactions.
	IFRIC 11 clarifies how to account for group-wide share-based payment transactions in the separate financial statements (and the sub-group consolidated financial statements) of the entity's subsidiaries and how to classify share-based payment transactions in which the entity does not issue treasury shares, but acquires them from third parties, or in which the share-based payment arrangement is settled by the entity's shareholders.
	If a parent grants the employees of its subsidiary its own equity instruments, this represents an equity-settled share-based payment transaction from the subsidiary's perspective. The grant by the parent is recognised as a capital contribution to the subsidiary.
	If a subsidiary grants its employees equity instruments of the parent, this represents a cash-settled share-based payment transaction from the subsidiary's perspective.
	For the purpose of classification as equity-settled, it is irrelevant whether the entity issues treasury shares, acquires them from third parties, or whether the share-based payment arrangement is settled by the shareholders.
Effective date:	Annual periods beginning on or after 1 March 2007. Earlier application is permitted.

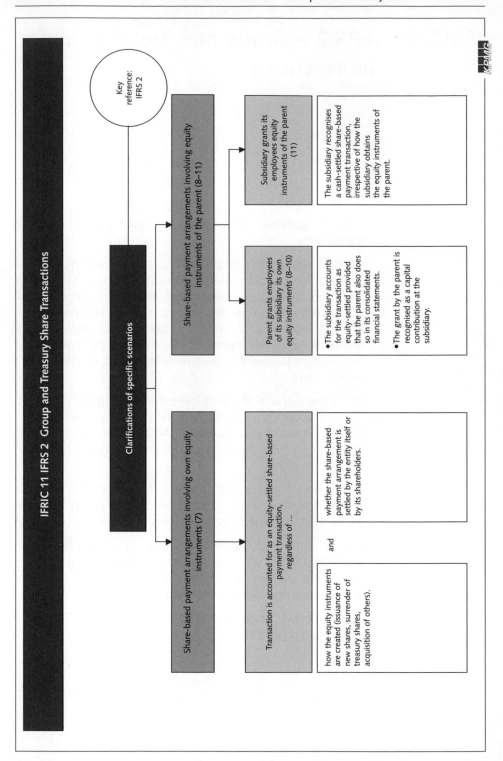

IFRIC 11 IFRS 2 Group and Treasury Share Transactions

Key reference: IFRS 2

Clarifications of specific scenarios

Share-based payment arrangements involving own equity instruments (7)

Transaction is accounted for as an equity-settled share-based payment transaction, regardless of ...

how the equity instruments are created (issuance of new shares, surrender of treasury shares, acquisition of others).

and

whether the share-based payment arrangement is settled by the entity itself or by its shareholders.

Share-based payment arrangements involving equity instruments of the parent (8–11)

Parent grants employees of its subsidiary its own equity instruments (8–10)

- The subsidiary accounts for the transaction as equity-settled provided that the parent also does so in its consolidated financial statements.
- The grant by the parent is recognised as a capital contribution at the subsidiary.

Subsidiary grants its employees equity instruments of the parent (11)

The subsidiary recognises a cash-settled share-based payment transaction, irrespective of how the subsidiary obtains the equity instruments of the parent.

KPMG

IFRIC 12 Service Concession Arrangements

References:	IFRS 1, IFRS 7, IAS 8, IAS 11, IAS 16, IAS 17, IAS 18, IAS 20, IAS 23, IAS 32, IAS 36, IAS 37, IAS 38, IAS 39
Core principles:	This Interpretation covers service concession arrangements that a government (grantor) grants to a private company (operator) to provide public services such as the construction, operation and maintenance of infrastructure and under which the government retains certain control rights. The Interpretation governs the recognition and measurement of the operator's rights, revenue and obligations arising from the arrangement.
	The operator recognises the right granted by the grantor as a financial asset to the extent that the operator has an unconditional right to receive payment of a specified consideration or settlement from the government. The operator recognises an intangible asset if it is granted a right to consideration that is contingent on the extent that the public uses the infrastructure. The operator may not recognise the infrastructure as property, plant and equipment.
	Revenue from the arrangements is recognised in accordance with IAS 11 or IAS 18 depending on whether it relates to the construction or operation of the infrastructure.
	Obligations to maintain the infrastructure are recognised in accordance with IAS 37.
Effective date:	Annual periods beginning on or after 1 January 2008. Earlier application is permitted.

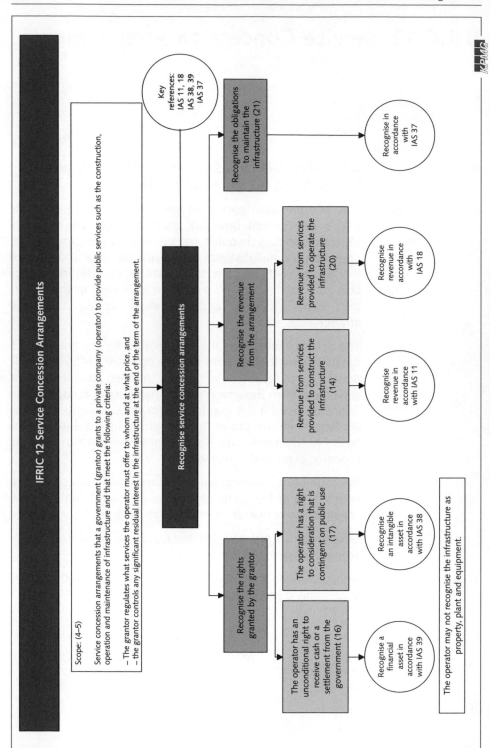

IFRIC 12 Service Concession Arrangements

Scope: (4–5)

Service concession arrangements that a government (grantor) grants to a private company (operator) to provide public services such as the construction, operation and maintenance of infrastructure and that meet the following criteria:

– The grantor regulates what services the operator must offer to whom and at what price, and
– the grantor controls any significant residual interest in the infrastructure at the end of the term of the arrangement.

Key references: IAS 11, 18 IAS 38, 39 IAS 37

Recognise service concession arrangements

Recognise the rights granted by the grantor

The operator has an unconditional right to receive cash or a settlement from the government (16)
→ Recognise a financial asset in accordance with IAS 39

The operator has a right to consideration that is contingent on public use (17)
→ Recognise an intangible asset in accordance with IAS 38

Recognise the revenue from the arrangement

Revenue from services provided to construct the infrastructure (14)
→ Recognise revenue in accordance with IAS 11

Revenue from services provided to operate the infrastructure (20)
→ Recognise revenue in accordance with IAS 18

Recognise the obligations to maintain the infrastructure (21)
→ Recognise in accordance with IAS 37

The operator may not recognise the infrastructure as property, plant and equipment.

IFRIC 13 Customer Loyalty Programmes

References:	IAS 8, IAS 18, IAS 37
Core principles:	This Interpretation applies to credits (award credits) that are granted under customer loyalty programmes involving an original transaction (sale transaction or rendering of services) and that can be redeemed by customers for free or discounted goods or services in the future.
	This Interpretation governs the recognition of award credits by the entity granting the award credits.
	Revenue from the original transaction must be separated into two components. The first, allocated to the award credits, shall be measured by reference to their fair value. The second is allocated to the goods or services supplied.
	If the entity granting the award credits itself supplies the goods or services to be redeemed, the component attributable to the award credits may not be recognised as revenue until the award credits are redeemed and the entity fulfils its obligations in respect of the awards.
	If the entity granting the award credits does not itself supply the goods or services to be redeemed, the following distinction must be made:
	If the entity collects the consideration for the award credits on its own account, the gross component attributable to the award credits must be recognised as revenue when it fulfils its obligations in respect of the awards. If the entity collects the consideration for the award credits on behalf of the entity ultimately supplying the awards, the difference between the fair value of the award credits and the amount payable to the entity ultimately supplying the awards must be recognised as revenue when the third party becomes obliged to supply the awards.
Effective date:	Annual periods beginning on or after 1 July 2008. Earlier application is permitted.

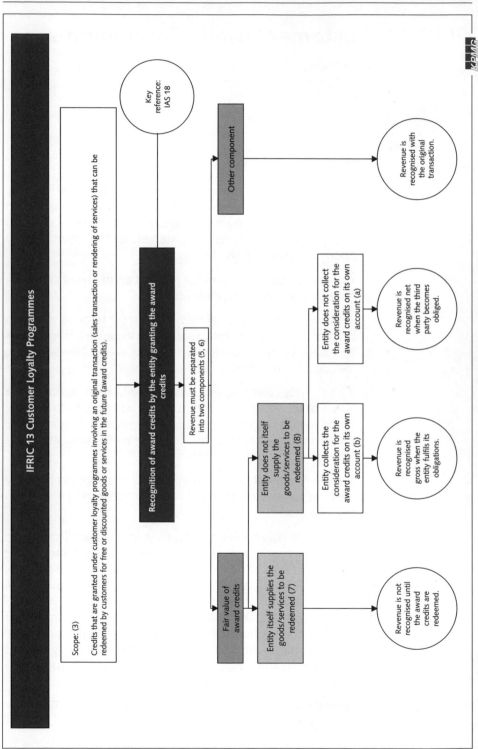

IFRIC 13 Customer Loyalty Programmes

Scope: (3)

Credits that are granted under customer loyalty programmes involving an original transaction (sales transaction or rendering of services) that can be redeemed by customers for free or discounted goods or services in the future (award credits).

Key reference: IAS 18

Recognition of award credits by the entity granting the award credits

Revenue must be separated into two components (5, 6)

Other component

Revenue is recognised with the original transaction.

Fair value of award credits

Entity itself supplies the goods/services to be redeemed (7)

Revenue is not recognised until the award credits are redeemed.

Entity does not itself supply the goods/services to be redeemed (8)

Entity collects the consideration for the award credits on its own account (b)

Revenue is recognised gross when the entity fulfils its obligations.

Entity does not collect the consideration for the award credits on its own account (a)

Revenue is recognised net when the third party becomes obliged.

IFRIC 14 IAS 19 – The Limit on a Defined Benefit Asset, Minimum Funding Requirements and their Interaction

References:	IAS 1, IAS 8, IAS 19, IAS 37
Core principles:	Under IAS 19.58, a defined benefit asset is measured at the lower of the amount determined under IAS 19.54 and the total of any cumulative unrecognised net actuarial losses and past service cost and the present value of any economic benefits available in the form of refunds from the plan or reductions in future contributions to the plan.
	The Interpretation clarifies that the terms and conditions of the plan and any statutory requirements must be considered when assessing whether such economic benefits may be regarded as available. It is sufficient if the benefit can be realised at some point during the life of the plan. The benefit therefore need not be realisable at the end of the reporting period. Additional requirements apply to the availability of benefits from refunds.
	The measurement of the economic benefit begins with a surplus (the fair value of plan assets less the present value of the defined benefit obligation) at the end of the reporting period and is modified differently depending on whether the economic benefits take the form of refunds from the plan or reductions in future contributions to the plan.
	In the case of the measurement of an economic benefit from reductions in future contributions to the plan, minimum funding requirements must also be taken into account if they are used to cover shortfalls in the future accrual of benefits.
Effective date:	Annual periods beginning on or after 1 January 2008. Earlier application is permitted.

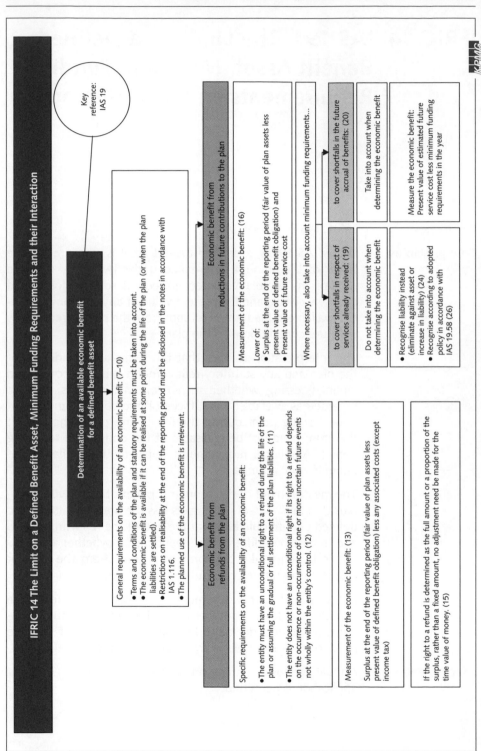

IFRIC 14 The Limit on a Defined Benefit Asset, Minimum Funding Requirements and their Interaction

Key reference: IAS 19

Determination of an available economic benefit for a defined benefit asset

General requirements on the availability of an economic benefit: (7–10)

- Terms and conditions of the plan and statutory requirements must be taken into account.
- The economic benefit is available if it can be realised at some point during the life of the plan (or when the plan liabilities are settled).
- Restrictions on realisability at the end of the reporting period must be disclosed in the notes in accordance with IAS 1.116.
- The planned use of the economic benefit is irrelevant.

Economic benefit from refunds from the plan

Specific requirements on the availability of an economic benefit:

- The entity must have an unconditional right to a refund during the life of the plan or assuming the gradual or full settlement of the plan liabilities. (11)
- The entity does not have an unconditional right if its right to a refund depends on the occurrence or non-occurrence of one or more uncertain future events not wholly within the entity's control. (12)

Measurement of the economic benefit: (13)

Surplus at the end of the reporting period (fair value of plan assets less present value of defined benefit obligation) less any associated costs (except income tax)

If the right to a refund is determined as the full amount or a proportion of the surplus, rather than a fixed amount, no adjustment need be made for the time value of money. (15)

Economic benefit from reductions in future contributions to the plan

Measurement of the economic benefit: (16)

Lower of:
- Surplus at the end of the reporting period (fair value of plan assets less present value of defined benefit obligation) and
- Present value of future service cost

Where necessary, also take into account minimum funding requirements...

to cover shortfalls in respect of services already received: (19)

Do not take into account when determining the economic benefit

- Recognise liability instead (eliminate against asset or increase in liability) (24)
- Recognise according to adopted policy in accordance with IAS 19.58 (26)

to cover shortfalls in the future accrual of benefits: (20)

Take into account when determining the economic benefit

Measure the economic benefit: Present value of estimated future service cost less minimum funding requirements in the year